Gendermaps

Also by John Money

Hermaphroditism: An Inquiry into the Nature of a Human Paradox, 1952

The Psychologic Study of Man, 1957

A Standardized Road-Map Test of Direction Sense (with D. Alexander and
  H. T. Walker, Jr.), 1965

Man and Woman, Boy and Girl: The Differentiation and Dimorphism of
  Gender Identity from Conception to Maturity (with A.A. Ehrhardt), 1972

Sexual Signatures (with Patricia Tucker), 1975

Love and Love Sickness: The Science of Sex, Gender Difference, and Pairbonding, 1980

The Destroying Angel: Sex, Fitness, and Food in the Legacy of Degeneracy
  Theory, Graham Crackers, Kellogg's Corn Flakes, and American Health
  History, 1985

Lovemaps: Clinical Concepts of Sexual/Erotic Health and Pathology, Paraphilia,
  and Gender Transposition in Childhood, Adolescence, and Maturity, 1986

Venuses Penuses: Sexology, Sexosophy, and Exigency Theory, 1986

Gay, Straight, and In-Between: The Sexology of Erotic Orientation, 1988

Vandalized Lovemaps: Paraphilic Outcome of Seven Cases in Pediatric Sexology (with M. Lamacz), 1989

Biographies of Gender and Hermaphroditism in Paired Comparisons: Clinical
  Supplement to the Handbook of Sexology, 1991

The Breathless Orgasm: A Lovemap Biography of Asphyxiophilia (with G.
  Wainwright and D. Hingsburger), 1991

The Kaspar Hauser Syndrome of "Psychosocial Dwarfism": Deficient Statural,
  Intellectual, and Social Growth Induced by Child Abuse, 1992

The Adam Principle: Genes, Genitals, Hormones, and Gender: Selected Read-
  ings in Sexology, 1993

The Armed Robbery Orgasm: A Lovemap Autobiography of Masochism (with
  R. Keyes), 1993

Sex Errors of the Body and Related Syndromes: A Guide to Counseling Children, Adolexscents, and their Families, 1994

Reinterpreting the Unspeakable: Human Sexuality 2000—The Complete Interviewer and Clinical Biographer, Exigency Theory, and Sexology for the
  Third Millennium, 1994

Edited by John Money

Reading Disability: Progress and Research Needs in Dyslexia, 1962

Sex Research: New Developments, 1965

The Disabled Reader: Education of the Dyslexic Child, 1966

Transsexualism and Sex Reassignment (with R. Green), 1969

Contemporary Sexual Behavior: Critical Issues in the 1970s (with J. Zubin),
  1973

Developmental Human Behavior Genetics (with W.K. Schaie, E. Anderson, and
  G. McClearn), 1975

Handbook of Sexology, volumes 1–5 (with H. Musaph), 1977

Traumatic Abuse and Neglect of Children at Home (with G. Williams), 1980

Handbook of Human Sexuality (with B.B. Wolman), 1980

Handbook of Sexology, volume 6 (with H. Musaph and J.M.A. Sitsen), 1988

Handbook of Sexology, volume 7 (with H. Musaph and M. Perry), 1990

The Handbook of Forensic Sexology: Biomedical and Criminological Perspectives (with J. Krivacska), 1994

Gendermaps

Social Constructionism, Feminism, and Sexosophical History

JOHN MONEY

CONTINUUM • NEW YORK

1995
The Continuum Publishing Company
370 Lexington Avenue, New York, NY 10017

Printed in the United States of America

Library of Congress Cataloging-in-Publication Data

Money, John, 1921–
    Gendermaps : social constructionism, feminism, and sexosophical
history / John Money.
        p.   cm.
    Includes bibliographical references and index.
    ISBN 0-8264-0852-4 (alk. paper)
    1. Sex.   2. Sex differences (Psychology)   3. Sex role—Political
aspects.   4. Feminist theory.   5. Homosexuality.   I. Title.
HQ23.M588   1995
    306.7—dc20

Dedicated to the world leader in the endocrinology of gender, my esteemed colleague and friend, Professor Louis Gooren, M.D.

Acknowledgments

The National Institute of Child Health and Human Development, Department of Health and Human Services, United States Public Health Service has supported the author in psychohormonal research for 38 years, currently under Grant # R25 HD-00325-38.

Sally A. Hopkins and William P. Wang worked industriously on this manuscript.

Contents

Introduction

U nless you stop to think about it, you will be taking it for granted that we human beings should be able to understand one another. Then the more you think, the more extraordinary will our mutual understanding seem to be, for we all exist within the confines of our own mental eggshells. Alone in there, the self is solipsistic. That is to say, it knows at first hand only its own ideas, images, and states of mind.

To inform others of our ideas, images, and states of mind, our only instruments of communication are our voices and our gestures—what we say and what we do. We expect that others will give the same meaning to our communications that we ourselves give to them. We assume, in other words, that the inhabitants of other eggshells are so sufficiently like ourselves that we may justifiably attribute to them principles of understanding identical with our own. Thus we assume that we all see red or green in the same way, that we all feel terror or pain in the same way, that we all feel hungry or sexy in the same way, that we all have the same sense of time and direction, that we all mean the same thing when we say we fall in love, or that we reach an orgasm, and so on. The miracle is that so often, when making these and countless other assumptions that other people will be just like ourselves, we are correct. Sometimes, however, we are not correct. Some people are tone deaf, for example. Others have a defective sense of direction. Some are dyslexic, or dyscalculic. Some are born without a sense of smell (anosmia) or a sense of pain (pain agnosia). Some are colorblind.

Colorblind and colorsighted people do not see colors in the same way, and neither can know exactly how the other experiences color. If they get into a dispute about, say, the color combinations in the clothes they are wearing, it may be interminable, for they will never see eye to eye.

Color blindness, either complete or partial, is far more prevalent in males than females. Thus, a couple may recurrently dispute color schemes, until their contentiousness ultimately destroys their relationship.

Men trying to understand women, and women trying to understand men are, on many issues, like the colorblind and the colorsighted trying to understand each other's recognition of color. Men are not able to get inside female solipsism, however, nor women inside of male solipsism. Consider, for example, the experience of sexual orgasm. Does a man's feel the same as a woman's, or not? No one, neither man nor woman, has ever been able to answer that question, and no one can. When a woman says she has fallen in love, do the words mean the same as when a man utters them, and is their experience the same? We may assume sameness, but not with a guarantee of certainty. When the question is about erotic arousal, the assumption of sameness is very tricky, for arousal in men is predominantly dependent on the eyes, and in women on the haptic or tactual skin senses.

Contentiousness between men and women begins often in faulty assumptions of identicality instead of disparity between masculinity and femininity. The popular cliché then is that they don't communicate. To be precise, they miscommunicate. They talk at cross-purposes. They are trapped within the solipsism of their own eggshells, from which neither can escape to understand the point of view of the other. Their miscommunication degenerates into a power struggle.

Power struggles affect men and women not only as couples, privately, but also as members of organizations, politically. Both types of power struggle constitute the subject matter of this book. It is a book about manhood and womanhood in conflict. It is also a book about the recent history of the new concept of **gendermaps** as applied to this conflict, and about the relationship between gender and gendermaps versus the old concept of sex. The term gendermaps was coined as a cognate of lovemaps for use in a paper delivered in 1992 at the Gender Identity and Development in Childhood and Adolescence International Conference, St. George's Hospital, London (Money, 1994a). It was subsequently used in the title of a paper delivered, also in 1992, at the Shanghai Conference of Sexology sponsored by the Shanghai Social Science Federation and the Asian Federation of Sexology in the Peoples' Republic of China, September 12–16, 1992 (Money, 1992–1993).

Our remote ancestors must have been extremely impressed with the difference between themselves as male and female to have gender-classified inanimate things also as male and female, or other (neuter). Perhaps it gave them confidence in putting the stamp of eternal verity on their stereotyping of much of human behavior as indelibly masculine or feminine. They and their gendered universe were at one with their deities, male and female. For those whose language would evolve into English, however, this universalization of gender was impermanent.

In modern English, only a few remnants of the attribution of gender to inanimate objects have survived, as in speaking of ships and cars and mother nature as she, and of countries as the motherland and fatherland. Otherwise gender, male and female, survived as an exclusive right of proper nouns and pronouns. At least it did so until 1955, when gender was given a new lease on life in the *Bulletin of The Johns Hopkins Hospital* (Money, 1955). Borrowed from pronouns, gender was therein applied to ways that people comport themselves in their roles as boys or girls, men or women. This new usage, medical at first, spread into the vernacular.

In a letter to the *New York Times* on December 27, 1990, Sidney Weinstein, editor-in-chief of the *International Journal of Neuroscience* lamented that "the term gender is increasingly used as a substitute for sex," and he questioned, "Does gender appear to reflect a greater sophistication, or reluctance to use a term with a possible indecent connotation?" Then, with disapproval, he quoted examples of gender used instead of sex: gender gulf; gender gap; and gender imbalance.

On January 18, the *New York Times* carried a reply to Weinstein by Sol Steinmetz, executive editor of Random House Dictionaries. "The use of the word gender to mean an individual's sex is well established in English and recognized by current dictionaries as standard. The term gender gap is itself firmly established; and it is clearer to speak of a gender imbalance than of a sex imbalance, which could be taken for a hormonal disorder . . . [gender] stresses the social and cultural over the biological differences between sexes and [its use] has steadily grown since about 1960."

The new use of gender was again deplored in a column by Robert S. McElvaine in the *Los Angeles Times*, July 23, 1993, under the heading, "What Ever Happened to S-x?" He quoted from a petition signed by half a million people and presented at a U.N. Conference on Human Rights which stated: "We demand gender violence to be recognized as a violation of human rights." He continued with the comment that "The violence complained of is all too real, but it is violence against a sex, not a gender." Then followed his "personal favorite, a recent headline: 'Gender of Blue Crabs Easy to Tell.'" Joking about blue crabs does not, however, come to terms with the fact that corporal violence against women (or men) is not synonymous with sexual violence against them. Corporal violence differs from violence that is specifically against the sex organs insofar as corporal violence is against not the gender, but the whole person. Violence against the whole person may happen to include injury of the sex organs. In other words it may incorporate sexual violence.

The single term, sex, signifies one's civil status, male or female, as declared on a birth certificate, tax form, driver's license, passport, or other document. The same term signifies also the morphology, function, and lustful activation of one's procreative organs. Ken and Barbie dolls are manufactured with nothing between their legs. They have no sex, but neutered though they be, they have plenty of discernible, even exaggerated gender as male or female, respectively. They symbolize a purified version of sex that has been rendered prudishly decent by being neutered and renamed gender. One concomitant of the neutering of gender has been a resurgence of the demonification of lust, a bizarre and unforeseen science-resistant cultural phenomenon of late twentieth-century politics and scholarship.

The credo upon which all genuinely scientific scholarship is constructed begins with: I believe in the empirical methodology of science whereby scientific principles are never safe from refutation, and scientific hypotheses are never safe from revision. In science nothing qualifies as absolute nor as existing in perpetuity. Scientific hypotheses are the creative insights of human minds. They are of the same order as the creative insights of artists and humanistic scholars, from which they differ only by the rigorously standardized methods of empirical testing to which scientific hypotheses are subsequently subjected. Like all creative insights, those of science are products of their time and place. They cannot come into existence except in the context of what went before them and of what presently surrounds them. With the passage of time, the explanations which they engender eventually become monuments to the human intellect as new explanations take their place.

There was a time, long gone, when the philosophy of science embraced the dogma that science discovers the eternal verities and absolute truths and laws of nature, and that it does so by dispassionately following the process of inductive reasoning. Early twentieth-century epistemology discredited that doctrine and replaced it with the doctrine of the sociology of knowledge, according to which scientific explanations are relative to the history and society in which they are generated. This relativism applies to particular explanations. It does not apply to the empirical methodology of science, per se.

As the twentieth century comes to a close, the epistemology of the sociology of knowledge has been reincarnated as social constructionism. The practitioners of social constructionism attack or deconstruct not only particular scientific explanations (and historical and literary explanations also), but also the entire methodology of science. Their principles and policies are those of piecemeal demolition. They have no epistemology of reconstruction. The outcome is the epistemology of transience. Deconstructed explanations have no durability. They survive only until they are, in turn, themselves attacked, deconstructed, and deprived of their fifteen Andy Warhol minutes of fame. They provide none of the stability for the continuation and expansion of knowledge that science provides. Although it is influenced by the society in which it is constructed, science is more than an ephemeral social construct, arbitrarily fabricated.

Sexual lust and gender have been arbitrarily cast asunder in the political rhetoric of feminism and in the scholarly rhetoric of social constructionism. Their severance has now become embodied in moral, legal, and vernacular rhetoric. The outcome of this embodiment, whether it will be permanent or time limited, cannot yet be foreseen.

· 1 ·

Lexical History and Constructionist Ideology of Gender

· 1 ·

Lexical History and Constructionist Ideology of Gender

Dictionaries and Gender

The terms *gender role*, *gender identity*, and *gender* in its usage as a synonym for sex, are nowadays ubiquitous in the print and electronic media, in social and biological science, and in medical, legal, political, and everyday discourse. They fit so snugly into the English vernacular that scholars and nonscholars alike use them on the assumption, by and large, that they have always been there. In the absence of accurate lexicographic documentation to the contrary, historians of a future generation might be expected to do the same. Their only alternative would be to make a major search of primary sources, decade by decade, until making the discovery that gender, as used at the end of the twentieth century, did not enter into general English usage, and thence by translation into other vernaculars, until early in the second half of this century.

Prior to that time, people had sex (from Latin, *secare*, to cut or divide), but not gender (from Latin, *genus*, race or kind). Sex belonged to the genitalia and procreation as male or female. Gender belonged to philology and grammar, for the classification of nouns, pronouns, and adjectives as masculine, feminine, or neuter. In the third and most recent edition of the unabridged *Webster's 3rd New International Dictionary of the English Language* (Merriam-Webster, 1986), the single word *sex* was given as one subsidiary meaning of *gender*—abridged but not otherwise changed from the entry in the original edition (G. & C. Merriam, 1930) which was:

> **gender**: sex, male or female. *Obsolete or Colloquial.*

The second edition (1989) of the *Oxford English Dictionary* (*OED*) also listed the single word *sex* as a subsidiary meaning of *gender*, and added the qualification, unchanged from the first edition (1933), "Now only jocular." Somewhat inconsistently, this second edition of the *OED* listed another subsidiary meaning of *gender* as follows. "In modern (especially feminist) use, a euphemism for the sex of a human being, often intended to emphasize the social and cultural, as opposed to the biological, distinctions between the sexes."

The second edition of the *OED* also lists under *gender* "special combinations" one of which is "gender-bender, slang, a person (especially a pop singer or follower of a pop cult) who deliberately affects an androgynous appearance by wearing sexually ambiguous clothing, make-up etc.; hence gender-bending; also gender-blender, gender-blending." Another special combination is "gender-gap" defined as "chiefly, U.S., the difference in (especially political) attitudes between men and women."

In its second edition, the *OED*'s first illustration of *gender* as "a euphemism for the sex of a human being" is taken from the book, *Sex in Society* by the British writer Alex Comfort (1963): "The gender role learned by the age of two years is for most individuals irreversible, even if it runs counter to the physical sex of the person."

Not only is this usage wrongly called a euphemism, but also its year, 1963, is eight years too late for the first appearance of the term *gender role*. Alex Comfort borrowed the term from the works of John Money who coined and defined it, as will be recognized "when the entries for *gender* and related terms come up for revision" in the third edition of the *OED* to be "published sometime early next century," according to a personal communication to William P. Wang (March 12, 1991), from the senior assistant science editor of the *OED*. Its first appearance in print was in the paper (Money, 1955) on "Hermaphroditism, gender and precocity in hyperadrenocorticism," published in the subsequently discontinued *Bulletin of the Johns Hopkins Hospital*. In this paper the word *gender* made its first appearance in English as a human attribute, but it was not simply a synonym for *sex*. With specific reference to the genital birth defect of hermaphroditism, it signified the overall degree of masculinity and/or femininity that is privately experienced and publicly manifested in infancy, childhood, and adulthood, and that usually though not invariably correlates with the anatomy of the organs of procreation.

Gender Role and Hermaphroditism

The origins and formulation of the concept of gender role in relation to research on hermaphroditism is so much a part of the present author's own scholarly and intellectual history that it is best told, autobiographically, in the first person, as follows.

It was as a graduate student in the Harvard psychological clinic that I first became directly acquainted with the phenomenon of hermaphroditism. This occurred under the tutelage of George E. Gardner, M.D., who presented a case in a seminar at the Judge Baker Guidance Center in Boston. This case set me on an academic course that would lead to a Ph.D. dissertation on *Hermaphroditism: An Inquiry into the Nature of a Human Paradox* (Harvard University, 1952) which allowed me to spend several hours interviewing and testing the youth in question. At that time, he was seventeen years old.

Diagnostically, his case was classified, according to the terminology of the era, on the basis of the presence of two undescended testes and no ovarian tissue, as one of male pseudohermaphroditism with the testicular feminizing syndrome, nowadays known as the androgen insensitivity syndrome. The external genitalia resembled a vulva with a clitoridean organ instead of a penis. Under the influence of female hormone normally secreted in males by the testicles, combined with inability of cells throughout the body to respond to male sex hormone, also secreted by the testicles, puberty had induced feminization of the secondary sexual characteristics of the body and no masculinization. Nonetheless the mind was oriented as that of a boy with a deformity, not as that of a girl. The child had been reared as a boy after a sex reannouncement from female to male early in infancy on the advice of a wrongly informed physician who had promised surgical and hormonal treatment in the teen-age years so as to allow the boy to become a man. By age fifteen he had been medically informed that he had the option of changing to live as a woman. It was an option too alien for him to contemplate. Romantically and emotionally he was aroused by girls, not boys. Later on, even though in his teens the perils of marriage seemed insurmountable, after qualifying as a physician he married a nurse. Together they established a sexual life, and adopted children.

This case pointed clearly toward the principle of a discontinuity between the development of the body, from prenatal life through puberty, as femininized, and the development of the mental life as masculinized, despite the restrictions imposed on genital masculinity by anatomical and hormonal femininity. Female anatomical and hormonal sex could not be said to cause what I then called a feminine "libidinal inclination, sexual outlook, and sexual behavior." It would require the evidence of nine other case reports with differing diagnoses, and of 248 cases from a medical literature review, to show also that masculine or feminine inclination, outlook, and behavior could not be automatically regulated by either the genetic or gonadal sex, nor by any other single anatomical or physiological variable of sex that could be identified in the data then available. Here are the actual words I wrote in the summary of my dissertation.

> The evidence of this review carries implications for that aspect of psychological theory that has to do with the origins and determinants of libidinal inclination, sexual outlook, and sexual behavior. In the face of the evidence it appears that the presence or lack of libido is clearly a function of the presence of sex hormones, regardless of their biochemical structure or their source of origin. The evidence weighs heavily, however, against the conception that individual erotic preferences—the direction and goal toward which libido is exercised—bear a direct or precise relationship to unlearned determinants. It does not appear feasible to ascribe these aspects of libido to a basis which is commonly described as constitutional or instinctive, organic or innate, unless it be specifically in terms of the localization of erotic sensation in the genitalia. The evidence weighs even more heavily against the conception that the more general aspects of sexual outlook and sexual behavior—in contrast to the specifically erotic aspects—bear a direct or precise relationship to unlearned determinants. In brief, it appears that psychosexual orientation bears a very strong relationship to teaching and the lessons of experience and should be conceived as a psychological phenomenon.

For the name of a single conceptual entity, there are too many words in the expression "libidinal orientation, sexual outlook, and sexual behavior as masculine or feminine in both its general and its specifically erotic aspects." The challenge to give a unitary name to the concept embodied in these many words became pressing after my case load of hermaphrodites studied in person had, after 1951, expanded from ten to sixty in Lawson Wilkins' Pediatric Endocrine Clinic at the Johns Hopkins Hospital, at which time a concise report of findings became essential.

The first step was to abandon the unitary definition of sex as male or female, and to formulate a list of five prenatally determined variables of sex that hermaphroditic data had shown could be independent of one another, namely, chromosomal sex, gonadal sex, internal and external morphologic sex, and hormonal sex (prenatal and pubertal), to which was added a sixth postnatal determinant, the sex of assignment and rearing (Money, 1955; Money et al., 1955). The seventh place at the end of this list was an unnamed blank that craved a name. After several burnings of the midnight oil I arrived at the term, gender role, conceptualized jointly as private in imagery and ideation, and public in manifestation and expression. Here is the paragraph in which the term, gender role first appeared in print (Money, 1955):

> Cases of contradiction between gonadal sex and sex of rearing are tabulated together with data on endogenous hormonal sex and gender role. The term gender role is used to signify all those things that person says or does to disclose himself or herself as having the status of boy or man, girl or woman, respectively. It includes, but is not restricted to sexuality in the sense of eroticism·

Then follow paragraphs in which gender role is compared with hormonal sex and morphologic sex. They lead up to a summary statement as follows:

> Chromosomal, gonadal, hormonal, and assigned sex, each of them interlinked, have all come under review as indices which may be used to predict an hermaphroditic person's gender—*his* or *her* outlook, demeanor, and orientation. Of the four, assigned sex stands up as the best indicator. Apparently, a person's gender role as boy or girl, man or woman, is built up cumulatively through the life experiences he encounters and through the life experiences he transacts. Gender role may be likened to a native language. Once ingrained, a person's native language may fall into disuse and be supplanted by another, but it is never entirely eradicated. So also a gender role may be changed or, resembling native bilingualism may be ambiguous, but it may also become so deeply ingrained that not even flagrant contradictions of body functioning and morphology may displace it.

I published the first formal definition of gender role as a footnote in a paper published later in 1955 conjointly with two colleagues (Money et al., 1955):

> By the term, gender role, we mean all those things that a person says or does to disclose himself or herself as having the status of boy or man, girl or woman, respectively. It includes, but is not restricted to sexuality in the sense of eroticism. Gender role is appraised in relation to the following: general mannerisms, deportment and demeanor;

play preferences and recreational interests; spontaneous topics of talk in unprompted conversation and casual comment; content of dreams, daydreams and fantasies; replies to oblique inquiries and projective tests; evidence of erotic practices and, finally, the person's own replies to direct inquiry.

The term, *gender identity*, had not at this time been coined.

Gender and Imprinting

In the academic climate of psychology and psychiatry of the 1950s, it was virtually universal to separate organic from psychogenic determinants, to explain psychogenic determinants predominantly in terms of one or another version of developmental learning theory, and to accept the idea that whatever is learned can be unlearned.

As a student, I had been steeped in the social anthropology of Franz Boas, Ruth Benedict, Margaret Mead, and Ernest Beaglehole, as well as in patterns of culture, and sociocultural learning. But I did not become a stimulus-response behaviorist, nor did I neglect the importance of yet to be discovered workings of the brain. By reason of my training, I was primed to be sensitive to the postnatal, mostly sociocultural determinants of gender role in hermaphrodites, but I was not about to sell out to social environmental determinism exclusively, as the following quotation indicates (Money et al., 1955).

> [My] studies of hermaphroditism have pointed very strongly to the significance of life experiences encountered and transacted in the establishment of gender role and orientation. This statement is not an endorsement of a simple-minded theory of social and environmental determinism. Experiences are transacted as well as encountered—conjunction of the two terms is imperative—and encounters do not automatically dictate predictable transactions. There is ample place for novelty and the unexpected in cerebral and cognitional processes in human beings.
>
> Novelty and unexpectedness notwithstanding, cerebral and cognitional processes are not infinitely modifiable. The observation that gender role is established in the course of growing up should not lead one to the hasty conclusion that gender role is easily modifiable. Quite the contrary! The evidence from examples of change or reassignment of sex in hermaphroditism, not to be presented here in detail (Hampson, 1955), indicates that gender role becomes not only established, but also indelibly imprinted. Though gender imprinting begins by the first birthday, the critical period is reached by about the age of eighteen months. By the age of two and one-half years, gender role is already well established.

The concept of behavioral imprinting was borrowed from the European school of animal ethology (Lorenz, 1952). As applied to gender role, one of the prime features of imprinting is that there is a critical or sensitive period in development, not before and not after, when it is able to take place. The timetable is phylogenetically programmed, as is also the releaser stimulus and the recognition response without which imprinting does not take place. Once it has taken place, there is no backtracking, not even to correct an error. There is an analogy here with anatomical differentiation of the embryo. The phylogenetic aspects of imprinting circumvent the false dichotomy between biology and social learning by uniting them at a critical phase of development.

The concept of gender role imprinting got professional exposure among psychiatrists when in 1956 the hermaphroditic research on which it was based was acknowledged by the Hofheimer Prize of the American Psychiatric Association. The paper published (Money et al., 1957) in response to that award, "Imprinting and the establishment of gender role," reached a still wider audience. Thenceforth, the concept of gender role took root in academia, but its published definition did not.

Gender: Role and Identity

In defining gender role as a unitary phenomenon, I had in mind the example of an actor whose greatness derives from his becoming the character whose role he portrays on the stage. Similarly, gender role is both interior and exterior. It belongs to the self, within, and concurrently manifests itself to others, without. This interior/exterior unity failed to hold its own in competition with the dichotomizing power of the academic zeitgeist in which the sociocultural is territorially separate from the psychological and psychobiological. Before long, gender role became dichotomized into interior and exterior. Gender role continued to apply to the exterior components, and gender identity became the term for the interior components of the dichotomy.

I first encountered the term *gender identity* early in the 1960s, in correspondence with Evelyn Hooker, Ph.D., famed for her research that discredited the official classification of homosexuality as a psychopathology (1957, 1958). She was associated with the University of California at Los Angeles (UCLA). Many years later, in a telephone call with the late Robert Stoller, M.D., also of UCLA, I learned that gender identity had been split off from gender role by the participants of a Los Angeles-based psychoanalytic group that met regularly from the late 1950s onward to discuss personal identity formation and other issues related to Stoller's investigation of the significance of hermaphroditism, transexualism, and gender for psychoanalytic theory. For them gender identity became an intrapsychic, neo-Freudian entity obtained developmentally by means of either male or female identification which, in psychoanalytic theory, is said to be primarily with a parent. Gender role became equated with cultural prescriptions and stereotypes of masculinity and femininity imposed by society and learned in childhood.

The relegation of gender role to social stereotyping and indoctrination was reinforced by yet another dichotomization, namely, that achieved by splitting off sex from gender. An early example is the title of Stoller's 1968 book, *Sex and Gender*. In the preface to this book, Stoller wrote: "The word sex in this work will refer to the male or the female sex and the component biological parts that determine whether one is male or female. . . . Those aspects of sexuality that are called gender are primarily culturally determined; that is, learned postnatally."

Although Stoller hedged his bets with various provisos and qualifications, others who followed him did not. Very soon it became an academic canon, repeated in a multitude of textbooks and journal articles, that sex is biological and what you're born with, whereas gender is socially learned and what you become. There was no place for sexual biology in the brain either prenatally determined hormonally, or postnatally determined developmentally in the psychobiology of learning and remembering.

The severance of biology and sex from gender and culture was adventitiously reinforced in November 1966 when the Johns Hopkins Hospital announced, in a press release (see appendix), the formation of a new clinic for the treatment of transexualism by sex reassignment. The clinic had been informally known as the sex change clinic, but at my instigation had been formally named the Gender Identity Clinic, a name that should have broadened its scope beyond transexualism to the manifold issues of gender identity. The narrower meaning, however, would win the day. Gender identity disorder became inseparably linked with transexualism. In the transexual, the gender identity, on the one hand, and the natal sex of the genitalia and the body morphology, on the other, are discordant with one another. This discordancy is commonly, though wrongly interpreted to signify that whereas the sex is biological, the gender identity is not, but is socially acquired or learned. Repeating a maxim from as far back as the 1850s, the transexual claims to have a woman's mind in a man's body, or a man's mind in a woman's body (Kennedy, 1988, chap. 7).

The great blind spot in this maxim is that it fails to recognize that the mind belongs to the brain which belongs to biology. Learning takes place in the brain. In neuroscience there is a vast experimental biology of learning and remembering. Another blind spot of the maxim is that it fails utterly to recognize the animal experimental and human clinical evidence of hormonal and maybe other yet undiscovered neurochemical, including neurosteroidal influences (Mellon, 1994) within the brain, especially prenatally, which act as precursors of subsequent masculinity or femininity of the body image and of gender identity formation in postnatal life.

Once the term *gender identity* had established its place in the language along with *gender role,* there was no point in not using both terms. In writing a glossary for the book, *Man and Woman, Boy and Girl: The Differentiation and Dimorphism of Gender Identity from Conception to Maturity* (Money and Ehrhardt, 1972), I defined each term as a reciprocal of the other, as follows:

> **gender identity**: the sameness, unity and persistence of one's individuality as male or female or ambivalent in greater or lesser degree, especially as it is experienced in self-awareness and behavior. Gender identity is the private experience of gender role, and gender role is the public expression of gender identity.

> **gender role**: everything that a person says and does, to indicate to others or to the self the degree in which one is male or female or ambivalent. It includes but is not restricted to sexual arousal and response. Gender role is the public expression of gender identity, and gender identity is the private experience of gender role.

In the grammatical construction of a sentence, gender identity and role as the subject require a plural verb, thus destroying any semblance of a unified concept. To overcome this obstacle, in the later years of the 1970s I devised a singular noun by using an acronym, G-I/R, for gender-identity/role. In the glossary of *Love and Lovesickness: The Science of Sex, Gender Differences, and Pair-Bonding* (Money, 1980), G-I/R is formally defined as follows.

> **gender-identity/role (G-I/R)**: gender identity is the private experience of gender role, and gender role is public manifestation of gender identity. Gender identity is the sameness, unity, and persistence of one's individuality as male, female, or ambivalent, in greater or lesser degree, especially as it is experienced in self-awareness and behavior. Gender role is everything that a person says and does to indicate to others or to the self the degree that one is either male or female, or ambivalent; it includes but is not restricted to sexual arousal and response.

Neutered Gender

After 1980, the term *gender* took on an independent lexical life of its own, or more correctly two lives of its own. One life was as an unabashed synonym for *sex*, male or female. For example, in a 1982 manuscript on sexual behavior the sex of reptiles, male or female, was initially referred to as their gender, though subsequently revised prior to publication. In a published paper (Shapiro, 1987) on hermaphroditic fish that change sex, disappearance of a female's male partner was said to "affect its gender identity," meaning that the female would become a male.

The second of *gender*'s independent lexical lives, the very antithesis of the first, specifically excluded biological sex and reproduction and signified male and female differences attributable to arbitrary cultural stereotypes and developmental socialization.

It was not until 1992, in the *American Heritage Dictionary* (3rd edition) that this second meaning of gender received straightforward lexical recognition. It did so as a **USAGE NOTE** subsumed under the entry for **gender** as follows.

> Traditionally, *gender* has been used primarily to refer to the grammatical categories of "masculine," "feminine," and "neuter"; but in recent years the word has become well established in its use to refer to sex-based categories, as in phrases such as *gender gap* and *the politics of gender*. This usage is supported by the practice of many anthropologists, who reserve *sex* for reference to biological categories, while using *gender* to refer to social or cultural categories. According to this rule, one would say *The effectiveness of the medication appears to depend on the sex* (not gender) *of the patient*, but *In peasant societies, gender* (not sex) *roles are likely to be more clearly defined*. This distinction is useful in principle, but it is by no means widely observed and considerable variation in usage occurs at all levels.

It was, in fact, not only in anthropology but also in all of social science, in particular among social psychologists and sociologists sooner than among anthropologists, that the practice evolved of using gender to refer to social or cultural categories. Social and developmental psychology had a long history of studying sex differences and sex roles. In this usage of sex, explicit procreative sexuality and eroticism were expressly excluded. Thus neutered sex prepared the way for neutered gender. The outcome is lexical confusion and redundancy. Masculine and feminine sex typing, sex roles and gender roles, sexual identity and gender identity, as well as sex differences and gender differences coexist in the literature. Compound terms like sex-role behavior, gender-role behavior, gender-role identity, and sex-role identity add further to the terminological redundancy and confusion.

The new usage of gender in social science not only divorced gender from biology, but also from the biology of procreation. Moralistically and politically, there was a hidden bonus in this divorce, for it allowed gender to be divorced also from the lustful carnality of the sex organs. Aphoristically, gender was located in the head, and sex in the pelvis. Gender was clean, and uncontaminated by dirty sex. It also circumvented the inescapable sex difference in procreation and pregnancy. Equal professional rights in the boardroom, irrespective of gender could be debated and demanded in public, whereas the genital-dependent reciprocity of equal sexual rights in the bedroom defied public disclosure. The politics of the woman's movement would not have survived the double entendre of a sex gap instead of a gender gap. Sex role also was a touchy word, as it veered too close to genital sex role. In the 1970s, the new neutered meaning of gender diffused rapidly through the political arena as well as through academia. Its diffusion in social science was accelerated by reason of its compatibility with the reincarnation of the old theory of sociocultural determinism, which eventually became absorbed by the epistemological theory of social constructionism. Its converse, essentialism, had formerly been named biological determinism. Essentialism versus social constructionism is currently the voguish reincarnation of nature versus nurture.

Attack on the Medical Model

In terms of the Hegelian dialectic, social constructionism is the antithesis and biological essentialism is the thesis. From the confrontation of thesis and antithesis, a synthesis should eventually emerge. The Marxist version of the Hegelian dialectic postulated that there must be a struggle or dispute between the proponents of the thesis and the antithesis. In the present instance this means a struggle between the proponents of biological essentialism (the thesis) and social constructionism (the antithesis) before a synthesis can occur. As reviewed by Leifer (1990), social constructionism began the struggle conversely as deconstructionism of the citadel of biological determinism, namely the citadel of the hated "medical model" of the biomedical establishment. The medical establishment in its entirety was not spared in Ivan Illich's *Medical Nemesis: The Expropriation of Health* (1976).

In the American social sciences scene of the early 1960s, deconstruction of the medical model began under the auspices of labeling theory (and in sociological sexology, scripting theory) which was the precursor of what would later be formally known as social constructionism. Psychiatry was the initial target.

Based on symptomology, not etiology, which continues to be primarily unknown, the psychiatric nosology has always been particularly vulnerable to a deconstructionist attack. The initial attack was launched from within by the psychiatrist, Thomas Szasz. His 1961 book is titled *The Myth of Mental Illness*. It was followed in 1963 by *Law, Liberty, and Psychiatry*. In these books, Szasz took the extreme position that there are no mental diseases analogous to physical diseases, only ideological, moral, or political divergences between patients and society at large, as well as between patients and health care providers with a vested interest in running asylums for the insane.

Szasz's contemporary in Britain was the psychiatrist R. D. Laing. Laing (1961, 1967) also was critical of using the medical model to define and explain the cause of psychiatric disorders. He explained schizophrenia as a sane response to the political and military insanity of mid-twentieth-century society.

Medical-sociological criticism of the medical model found a voice in the 1960s in California in the person of the sociologist, Erving Goffman, who wrote on the stigmatizing effects of being encumbered with a diagnosis and consigned to an institution. He published *Asylums: Essays on the Social Situation of Mental Patients and Other Inmates* (1961); and *Stigma: Notes on the Management of Spoiled Identity* (1963).

From within the ranks of American sociological sexology in the first half of the 1970s another theory of dissent against the medical model arose under the name of social scripting. Its proponent, the sociologist, John Gagnon, together with the psychologist, William Simon, published *Sexual Conduct: The Social Sources of Human Sexuality* (1973). In this book variant forms of sexual behavior were said to be not simply socially labeled, but actually acquired by learning from social scripts. Gagnon in 1974 published a follow-up volume, *Human Sexualities*.

Antagonism toward the medical model adventitiously led American social sciences and social psychiatry toward an alliance with French philosophical scholarship that had its roots in phenomenology as originally expounded by Husserl (1900; Eng. trans., 1970) and Heidegger (1927; Eng. trans., 1962) in reaction to the logical positivism of Wittgenstein (1921; Eng. trans., 1981); Ayer (1935; Eng. trans., 1950); and Popper (1959). Phenomenology gave way to the philosophy of existentialism of Sartre (1943; Eng. trans., 1953) and de Beauvoir (1952), with its doctrine of truth as a contingency of the person defining it. Existentialism, in turn, gave way to epistemological constructionism according to which truth is not absolute but is contingent on the language used to express it.

Epistemological constructionism arose in part as a reaction against the linguistic structuralism of Ferdinand de Saussure (1916; Eng. trans., 1966). The poststructural model discards the idea of a fixed connection between the source, a sign (the signifier), and the meaning or message that it signifies, and replaces it with the idea that the meaning or message is an attribute of the words that convey it.

According to the epistemology of constructionism, each truth that words express is socially constructed. That is to say, a truth is an expression of a social or political ideology endorsed by those who have the power and the authority to impose it on others and to enforce their acquiescence and agreement. In other words, truth is the same as belief, and has no claim to be exclusive or certain.

There have been three main applications of epistemological constructionist thinking in what is now known as postmodern scholarship. Jacques Lacan has applied it to psychoanalysis and a reinterpretation of Freud (1982). Jacques Derrida has applied it to literature and the deconstruction of contemporary literary criticism (1967; Eng. trans., 1978, 1967; Eng. trans., 1976). Michel Foucault has applied it to cultural and historical philosophy and the deconstruction of traditionally accepted explanations.

In the late seventies and early eighties, Foucault and Derrida both taught part of each year at an American university, Derrida at Yale, and Foucault at Berkeley, thus ensuring that the ideas of each would diffuse into American scholarship. Foucault had published a historical debunking of the medical model of insanity in *Madness and Civilization: A History of Insanity in the Age of Reason* (1961; Eng. trans., 1965); and a more general debunking of medical power in *The Birth of the Clinic; An Archaeology of Medical Perception* (1963; Eng. trans., 1973). *The History of Sexuality, Vol. I: An Introduction* was translated into English in 1978. In this volume, Foucault depicted the medical model of sexuality as an instrument of oppression, of the enforcement of political power and of supremacist male sexual domination.

As compared with social labeling theory and social scripting theory, Foucault's social constructionist theory offered an additional postulate, namely that, although social labels, scripts, or constructs may seem to represent eternal verities, they are actually arbitrary ideologies of oppression contrived or maintained by the established elite to guarantee their own privilege, status, and power over those whom they exploit.

Foucault's social constructionism had a ready-made audience among opponents of the medical model, especially licensed or certified non-M.D. mental health professionals. From the seventies onward, they had witnessed the gradual erosion of Freudian influence in American psychiatry and its replacement by biological and pharmacological psychiatry. Among health professionals, psychiatrists commanded the highest fees. They alone could prescribe medicational treatment which is less time-consuming than the talking treatment of psychotherapy. As costs escalated and insurance companies economized under the aegis of managed care, lesser paid, non-M.D. professionals replaced M.D. professionals as providers of psychotherapy and counseling, generically characterizable as talking treatment. For them the antibiomedical doctrine of social constructionism was made to order. It was made to order also for other opponents of the biomedical model, namely, the so-called antiessentialists of the established social sciences. For them, social constructionism was no more than a cosmetic change of name for sociocultural theory, social learning theory, and labeling theory. For their kin in the newly established divisions of feminist, ethnic, gay, and other minority studies in the humanities, however, social constructionism gave a name to a newly claimed brand of politically correct scholarship, and Foucault became their high priest.

Social constructionism was quickly absorbed into the radical antiestablishment rhetoric of the militant wing of the feminist movement and of the movement for gay and lesbian rights (Stein, 1992). The great appeal of social constructionism was that it provided justification for rebellion against the enemy, who could be variously named the scientific, religious, legal, or political establishment, the patriarchal system, Judeo-Christian morality, the medical profession, gender bias, racial prejudice, or endemic homophobia.

Declassification of Homosexuality

For gay rights activists and opponents of biomedical essentialism, the listing of homosexuality as mental illness in the first and second editions of the Diagnostic and Statistical Manual (DSM) of the American Psychiatric Association (APA) was a clear example of long-standing homophobic, ideological bias masquerading as medical science. Gay rights activists were ready to challenge this bias after the success of the gay and drag queen riot in 1969 protesting the police invasion of a gay bar, Stonewall Inn, in New York's Greenwich Village. With the support of a group of psychiatrists, gay activists confronted the APA with a demand to remove homosexuality from its manual. In 1973 the upshot was that the Board of Trustees of the APA voted to declassify homosexuality as an illness by excluding it from DSM-II and the upcoming third edition of the APA Manual, DSM-III (Slovenko, 1980, p.195; Nardi et al., 1994). The decision was not unanimously accepted by the APA membership and so was put to the vote in a referendum in 1974. The declassification of homosexuality was endorsed. Unless it was ego dystonic, homosexuality was reclassified not as a psychiatric pathology, but as a sexual orientation, variant, or preference.

The outcome of the APA referendum was proof positive, writ large for all to behold, that a mental illness had been socially constructed, and could be deconstructed and abolished by ballot. Admittedly, homosexuality was a well chosen example for it had a history, in ancient Greece, of not being an illness, but a socially viable option. In early Christian teaching, homosexuality had been outlawed as sin. In the civil law, under the Byzantine Emperor Justinian it had been decreed like adultery to be a civil crime and punishable by death (Boswell, 1980). At the end of the nineteenth century it began to be transferred from criminology to medicine, where it was claimed as a psychiatric illness and alleged to be treatable. When declassified in 1974, it changed from being an illness to being once again a socially viable sexual variant. Homosexuality, like left-handedness or color blindness, became a minority characteristic not to be classified in terms of sickness or health, but simply as being different from the sexuality of the majority, and deserving of moral tolerance, not intolerance.

One of the defining characteristics of any illness is that it is a state of existence intolerable to the person undergoing it, or intolerable to others in contact with that person, or both. Some psychiatric illnesses, like depression, are intolerable to the person afflicted, whereas others, like delusions of grandeur and paraphilic sexuality, are primarily intolerable chiefly to those closely involved with, or tyrannized by the afflicted person. Illnesses that are defined only by the intolerance of others may, like homosexuality, justifiably be candidates for being voted out of existence.

The politics of the gay liberation movement responsible for the psychiatric declassification of homosexuality shares with the women's movement the political correctness of separating carnal sex from noncarnal gender. In the case of homosexuality, the dichotomy is represented as a separation of sexual preference (also referred to as sexual object choice) from gender identity and gender role. Sexual preference signifies the sex of the partner, male or female, with whom one engages in sexuoerotic activities. It carries with it a polite evasiveness with respect to the carnal details of genitoerotic roles and practices. In addition, sexual preference signifies a philosophical position of free will and moral choice which gives social constructionists a free hand to claim that homosexuality, and vice versa, heterosexuality are nonbiological products of socialization.

In much of the professional jargon regarding homosexuality, gender identity signifies one's self-definition as man or woman. This simplified polarity does not allow for the concept of variable degrees of homosexual gender identity. Instead, it dichotomizes homosexuals as having either a masculine or a feminine gender identity. One outcome of this false polarity is that male-to-female, and female-to-male transposition of gender identity has been made falsely synonymous with its most extreme degree, namely, transexualism with sex reassignment. The other outcome of this false polarization is that it has no place for partial transpositions of gender identity which differentiate the degree of the macho from the effeminate in male homosexuals, and correspondingly of the butch from the femme in lesbians.

Gender identity's terminological twin is gender role. In the professional jargon regarding homosexuality, gender role signifies one's social comportment as manly or womanly, but only in situations that do not disclose one's sexuoerotic orientation and genital practices as homosexual or lesbian. As in the case of gender identity, the sexuoerotic and the nonsexuoerotic components of gender role are falsely polarized. This faulty polarity leads to the faulty assertion that a stereotypically macho man may have a sexual preference for men without being defined as having a transposition of the masculine gender stereotype which, by definition, he does in fact have, albeit restricted to genital eroticism and partner matching. Such a restricted transposition may be limited to being able to perform sexually only or predominantly with a man, and to be able to fall in love only with a man. For some heterosexual males, performance sexually with another male is an absolute impossibility. The bisexual is able to respond not only to a man but also to a woman. Women are correspondingly similar.

For both men and women, the separation of homosexual sex from homosexual gender is further achieved in the agenda of the homosexual rights movement by eliminating the very word *sex*, as in *homosexual*, replacing it with *gay* and *lesbian* instead. Although it is no doubt politically expedient to deconnect gender role from explicitly carnal sexuality and eroticism in the gay and lesbian rights movement, it is not scientifically defensible to do so.

· 2 ·

New Phylism Theory, Male and Female Gender

Polarity
Male/Female Bipotentiality
Parameters of Sex-Shared/Threshold Dimorphism
Flirtation
Academic and Career Achievement

· 2 ·

New Phylism Theory,
Male and Female Gender

Polarity

Social constructionism is postmodernism's name for the nurture pole of the nature/nurture polarity. At the other pole, essentialism is postmodernism's name for nature. In social constructionist scholarship, essentialism carries a somewhat pejorative connotation which signifies that a given attribute, like masculinity or femininity, has its origin in a fixed essence, and is preordained genetically, innately, or constitutionally. By contrast, social constructionism postulates that the same attribute originates adventitiously as an artifact of societal or cultural history.

In some branches of social science and humanities it is politically correct and in vogue to be self-declared as a social constructionist. There are no self-declared essentialists, however. The nearest approximation would be among those who look for so-called universals of human nature (Brown, 1991). Exclusive essentialists exist as academic ghosts set up by social constructionists to be their adversaries.

The postmodern polarization of essentialism and social constructionism is as obsolete as its forerunner, namely the polarization of nature versus nurture. Thinking people have long recognized the integrative unity and interdependence of what is contributed to development from each side of the polarity. One cannot exist without the other.

Even in its most rabid form, social constructionism can only ignore, but not refute the evidence that there are some essential and universal differences between masculine and feminine as, in particular, in the reciprocal roles of males and females in procreation and the female role in breast feeding. Conversely, there is no denying that some aspects of masculine and feminine roles, such as the styles of apparel and fashions in personal adornment, are not essential and not universal, but are socially dictated and regionally variable.

In individual development, the analogy between masculine/feminine role dimorphism and native language has already been mentioned. The ability to acquire a human language is transmitted in the human genome, but the actual language acquired is transmitted socially by listening and talking. The same principle applies to masculine/feminine role dimorphism. The ability is phylogenetically given, whereas the actuality is ontogenetically given. That which is phylogenetic is given to each member of our species and is shared by everyone as part of our species' history. That which is ontogenetic is unique to each individual history. In personal development, from conception onward, that which is individually unique is superimposed on that which is universally shared.

The basic building blocks of segments or sequences of behavior belong to all human beings, male or female, not as products of social construction, but simply by reason of our evolutionary heritage as members of the human species. They have been variously named as instincts, reflexes, and (in ethology) innate recognition and releasing mechanisms or fixed action patterns; but they have lacked an overall generic name. To overcome that lack I settled on the term phylism (Money, 1983). This term is derived from the Greek, *phylon* (Latin *phylum*) and is related to phyletic and phylogeny. A phylism is defined as a unit or building block of our existence that belongs to us as individuals through our heritage as members of our species. Commenting on this definition, Feierman (1990, p. 458) wrote:

> A phylism is compatible with the ethological definition of a unit of adaptive functioning. This definition would make the relationship of a phylism to function similar to the relationship of a fixed-action pattern to (behavioral) structure. Fixed-action patterns change in function phylogenetically but maintain structural integrity, whereas phylisms change in structure phylogenetically but maintain functional integrity. Although it is likely that fixed-action patterns are under the control of the same or similar DNA on homologous chromosomes in closely related species, this mechanism is unknown and unlikely for phylisms. The mechanism of

genetic transmission through phylogeny for a trait that is defined on the basis of function is yet to be fully understood. Nevertheless, the concept of a phylism seems to fill a certain need at this time inasmuch as there is no other term that means the same thing.

A great many phylisms retain their original Anglo-Saxon names, some of which are considered vulgar. Without the dignity of names derived from Latin and Greek, perhaps they become stigmatized as unworthy of learned consideration. Their vernacular names include: breathing, coughing, sneezing, hiccuping, drinking, swallowing, biting, chewing, pissing, shitting, fucking, laughing, crying, walking, grasping, holding, sweating, touching, hurting, tasting, smelling, hearing, and seeing. The complete list has not been counted. Other phylisms have Latinate names, like thermoregulation, salt regulation, and immunoregulation. Still others exist that have yet to be named, or that have been named only recently, for example, pairbonding and troopbonding.

The majority of phylisms, like breathing, coughing, sneezing, and so on, are neither masculine nor feminine, but are sex-shared. Remarkably few are exclusively masculine or exclusively feminine. One obvious example of exclusivity is that men do not lactate and breast feed, whereas women do.

Women also menstruate and, in synchrony with the menstrual cycle, they may have episodic mood swings and intrapelvic cramping for which there is no exact parallel cyclicity in men. Correspondingly, despite talk about a male climacteric, there is no exact male parallel of menopausal phenomena like unexplained crying spells and hot flashes that are female experiences, except as a possible sequel to the removal of the testicles.

At puberty, a phylism that is typical of males but not females is the ejaculation of semen while asleep, often with an accompanying erotic dream, the so-called wet dream. Although some girls report a pubertal history of erotic dreams that culminate in orgasm while asleep, the prevalence of such dreams in girls as compared with boys is, according to current data, low.

Many phylisms are categorized as sex-shared but threshold dimorphic. That is to say, they are present in both males and females, but are more readily triggered in one sex than the other. For example, an adolescent boy has a lower threshold for erotic arousal (he is more readily aroused) in response to sexy pin-up pictures than does an adolescent girl. The girl, although not erotically indifferent to what she sees, is more dependent than is the boy on tactual rather than visual stimuli to get actually "turned on" erotically. The girl and the boy both respond to visual as well as to tactual erotic stimuli, and vice versa, but with divergent thresholds for becoming aroused by and responsive to each type of stimulation.

When the same phylism is shared by males and females, but with a different threshold for its expression, it is possible that the divergent threshold levels are preset as early as in perinatal life when steroidal sex hormones organize bipotential brain regions and pathways to differentiate as predominantly either male or female. From animal experiments, there is abundant evidence that such organization does indeed take place (reviewed in Sitsen, 1988, and in Gerall et al., 1992). Corresponding evidence that the same applies to human beings is not experimental, but clinical. It comes from spontaneously occurring syndromes, notably of prenatal hormonal anomalies associated with hermaphroditism and related birth defects of the sex organs (reviewed in Money, 1986; 1994b).

Male/Female Bipotentiality

The principle whereby the initial bipotentiality of the developing mammalian brain differentiates into either masculine or feminine is cumulative. The embryo's priority is to develop from its bipotential state as a female. Without gonads and/or without gonadal hormones, embryonic and fetal development of the body, including the brain, is as for a female, irrespective of chromosomal sex. For male development something must be added, and that something is the male hormone, testosterone, or one of its metabolic derivatives. Paradoxically, for masculinization of some brain pathways, notably in the hypothalamus, testosterone must be enzymatically converted (aromatized) within the cell that uses it into estradiol, which elsewhere in the body acts as a feminizing hormone.

In human beings as compared with four-legged laboratory mammals, it is less likely that brain masculinization takes place prenatally or perinatally than that it does do in the first few weeks after birth. Between the ages of two and twelve weeks, in male infants there is a surge of male hormone secreted by the testicles into the blood stream. After reaching the level of puberty, it then subsides completely until the onset of puberty. There is no corresponding surge of ovarian hormone in female infants. However, there may be a demasculinizing effect induced in infant females by the neurotransmitter, serotonin (see chap. 6).

In prenatal life, female development may be masculinized, or male development demasculinized by, respectively, an excess or a deficiency of masculinizing hormone. Either error may be brought on by hormonal malfunction originating within the fetus, the placenta, or the mother.

Maternal hormonal malfunction may originate in a disorder of the mother's own endocrine system, including a hormone-secreting tumor, or it may be induced by hormone-containing medication inadvertently or erroneously prescribed.

Other maternal medications, for instance those containing barbiturates, may cross the placenta and adversely influence the level of hormones reaching the baby's brain (O.B. Ward, 1992, chap. 6). Perhaps there are also other toxic substances, as yet undiscovered, that the mother eats or breathes and that influence the degree of brain masculinization or demasculinization in the baby. Maternal stress is another factor. In rat experiments it has been unequivocally shown that maternal stress hormones from the adrenocortical glands exert a demasculinizing effect on unborn male pups (I.L. Ward, 1992, chap. 5).

By interpolating from animal experimental findings, it is evident that unwanted degrees of prenatal and neonatal brain masculinization or feminization, and likewise demasculinization or defeminization, do have an effect on various types of sex-shared/threshold-dimorphic behavioral phylisms or, in the language of ethology, units of adaptive functioning. The ratio of masculine sexual mounting to feminine sexual presentation (lordosis) is one example.

For the usual ethical reasons, there is no experimentally manipulated human evidence of masculinized or demasculinized changes in brain structures, nor in the neurohormonal chemistries of their function. The evidence is behavioral only, and it is derived from clinical observation in so-called experiments of nature, not contrived experiments. The parameters of sex-shared/threshold-dimorphic phylismic behavior in human beings have been provisionally classified (Money, 1980) as follows.

- General kinesis: muscular activity and the expenditure of energy, especially in vigorous outdoor, athletic, and team sport pursuits.
- Competitive rivalry and assertiveness for higher rank in the dominance hierarchy of childhood.
- Roaming and territorial boundary mapping or marking.
- Territorial defense against intruders and predators.
- Guarding and defense of the young.
- Nesting or homemaking.
- Parental care of the young, including doll play.
- Sexual positioning: mounting and thrusting versus presenting and enveloping.
- Erotic arousal: dependence on visual versus tactual stimuli.

Parameters of Sex-Shared/ Threshold Dimorphism

General Kinesis: Kinesis (from Greek, *kinein*, to move) signifies coordinated muscular movement of the limbs and mobilization of the whole body in motoric energy expenditure, as in walking, running, jumping, climbing, swimming, swinging, riding, throwing, lifting, digging, hitting, grabbing, pushing, and shoving, singly or combined in complex athletic activities. From early infancy onward, boys on the average have a higher level of motoric pursuits than do girls who, on the whole, have a higher level of sedentary pursuits. Although this male/female discrepancy may continue through adolescence into young adulthood, it progressively evens out with advancing age.

Competitive Dominance: Like other primates that live in troops, human beings live affiliatively in groups in which dominance is hierarchical. Among children, dominance rivalry varies according to the age and sex composition of the group. The older usually have the advantage over the younger, and boys over girls. In same-age, same-sex peer groups, rivalry for dominance among boys is more likely to take a muscular form of rivalry, especially in physical fighting and bullying, whereas among girls it is more likely to take a devious form of rivalry, especially in verbal dispute and deception.

In both boys and girls, the maintenance of a position of dominance requires forming same-sex power alliances. In addition dominance in one sex may be reinforced by finding favor with the dominant leaders of the other sex. In adolescence and adulthood, the maintenance of dominance is related especially to success in outbidding rivals for an envied sexual partner. In men, the checkbook and the investment account may become a weapon more powerful than physical combat.

Roaming: Phyletically, roaming is related to mapping the boundaries of the home territory, either as a deterrent to intruders, or as an attractant to a mate. Olfactory territorial marking is a feature of some four-legged mammalian species. The marking odor is secreted only by the male, either in the urine or from special glands under the chin or tail, and is testosterone dependent.

Olfactory boundary marking is not a feature of primate species. Rather, the limits and markers of the home range are recognized visually. The eyes take over from the nose. There is no clearcut primate evidence as to whether there is a male/female threshold difference in establishing and maintaining the boundary limits of the home range.

However, there is some human evidence that on the average there is a predominance of females over males who have a poor direction sense and who are not adept at giving directions or reading a map. Among infants and young children, boys more than girls are given to roaming unescorted away from home base, getting lost, and maybe losing their lives. Historically men have had a monopoly on exploring and confronting unknown dangers in unknown territories.

Territorial Defense: The maintenance of territorial boundaries entails excluding intruders that encroach upon and try to occupy the home range. It also entails defending the troop against marauding predators that prey upon its members. Among troop-living primate species, the defense of the troop against territorial intruders and predators (or vice versa, being killed as an intruder or predator) commonly devolves upon young adult males. Historically, although not inevitably, this has also been the case in the history of human warfare.

Some primate intruders are young adult males of the same species that have left their own troop to search for a female partner either by invading and taking over the invaded troop, or by recruiting females into a new troop of their own. Correspondingly, by ancient human custom, it has been the man who takes a bride.

Although there are species in which young adult females leave the home troop in search of a mate, preponderantly in primate species the young adult males are the ones that leave home. They then become invaders to be attacked by the young males of another troop, and driven out. Thus, males in many if not all primate species are phyletically programmed with an easily surmounted threshold for engaging in territorial defense against intruders or predators. The young adult male threshold for defense of the territory and the troop is preponderantly lower and more easily surmounted than is that of the young adult female.

Defense of Young: In professional psychology as well as in popular usage, aggression is not often differentiated on the basis of the circumstances that provoke it, the manner of its expression, or the sex of the opponent. Among carnivores, males and females may share either equally or disproportionately in killing for food. Among mammalian species that are noteworthy for mating rivalry, fighting is between rival males. In primate troops noted for territorial defense against intruders, marauders, and predators, the defenders are predominantly young adult males. Among primate as well as subprimate species, however, maternal defense of the young is fierce. The threshold for its elicitation is lower and less resistant in the female than the male. In defense of the young, the male may need to be prompted by the female. There is one proviso, however. Under certain circumstances, some females as well as some males abuse and destroy their young, rather than protect and defend them.

Nesting: "The boys all rushed for the doll buggies on wheels and pushed them wildly about, colliding. The girls picked up doll babies with their wrappings and made safe baby-care dens for them." So in the 1970s I wrote as an observer of three-year-olds at the nursery school of an exclusively Aboriginal township on the north central coast of Arnhem Land in the Northern Territory of Australia. The children were members of the first generation who had come in from walkabout in the bush and who had access to such children's toys. Nonetheless, they exhibited the same type of boy/girl play differential as is found worldwide.

In the older juvenile years, interest in homemaking in boys is predominantly structural and runs to tree houses, forts, cabins, club houses, and hideaways. Their occupancy is mostly for boys only. Girls are predominantly committed to finding a more or less secluded indoor or outdoor location to use as a den in which to play house undisturbed, and to rehearse with dolls the day-to-day routines of infant care. Neatness is a characteristic of girls' more than boys' house play.

In adulthood, men and women are more likely to complement rather than replicate each others' activities in homemaking. Traditionally, men construct and repair homes, and women arrange the decor and furnishings. More men than women are inclined to arrange furniture around the perimeter of a room, whereas more women than men are inclined to utilize the central space also. Male and female homemaking traditions are reversed in the case of some gay men and lesbian women.

Parentalism: Except for the obvious feminine exclusivity of postdelivery suckling at the breast, men can substitute for women in performing the parental functions of retrieving, protecting, cuddling, rocking, clinging and otherwise attending to the requirements of young infants. In subhuman primate species it can be shown that males, although they may be ponderously slow in responding to the cajoling of young infants, do eventually respond by holding and grooming them, and warning strangers to keep their distance. The stimulus-response interval in females is, by contrast, momentarily rapid. In prepubertal females it is also much faster than in males.

As in other troop-living primates, human parental care like parental protection of the young is phylismically sex-shared although threshold-dimorphic. The ear of the sleeping single-parent father, for instance, becomes as exquisitely attuned to the nocturnal stirrings of the baby as does that of the mother, whereas the dual-parent father stays soundly asleep while the mother wakens.

As children grow older, despite divergences in parental role, the father-child and the mother-child bonds do not necessarily differ in intensity, although father-daughter and mother-son bonding may have selective intensity.

Sexual Positioning: Sexual mounting is conventionally defined as male behavior, and sexual presenting (lordosis) as female behavior, but in fact male and female animals each may engage in both types of behavior. Infant male and female rhesus monkeys, for example, in their sexual rehearsal play engage in mounting and presenting irrespective of their own sex or the sex of the partner. Provided they are not deprived of such play, they eventually become appropriately adept at male/female matching, and at reciprocally correct copulatory positioning (Money, 1988a, pp. 64–65).

From experimental animal studies the evidence is that prenatal brain hormonalization influences whether subsequent sexual positioning will be predominantly either mounting or presenting. This influence is itself, in turn, influenced by postnatal socialization, especially as experienced in reciprocal infantile and juvenile sexual rehearsal play. For example, ram lambs that are sex-segregated on farms for the first year of life engage in sexual rehearsal play and continue being interested sexually in rams instead of ewes in heat when they reach maturity at a year of age (Mathur and Joshi, 1994; Mathur et al., 1994; Perkins and Fitzgerald, 1992; Perkins et al., 1995).

In human childhood, the tactual stimulation of shared body contact, as in being cuddled, caressed, or hugged, takes developmental precedence over explicit genital self-stimulation, which in turn takes precedence over explicit genital positioning play with a partner. Juvenile sexual rehearsal play is not discriminatory with respect to male/female matching to begin with, but it becomes more so with advancing age as reciprocal genital-digital play gives way, by age eight, if not sooner, to mounting and presenting play. Male/female matching in copulatory positioning begins by being bipotential for an unspecified period of time, after which it usually, but not invariably becomes progressively monopotential. Monopotentiality is heterosexual in a majority of cases, and homosexual in a minority.

Prenatal/neonatal hormonal determinants and postnatal social determinants of a long-term bipotential or monopotential outcome, whether heterosexual or homosexual, are subject to ongoing research. So also is the possibility of a determinant encoded in the genome (Hamer et al., 1993). The research task is all the more complex in that sexual positioning in the human species involves not only the genital orifices, but also the oral and anal.

Erotic Arousal: Among four-legged mammals there are many species in which the male nose is the organ of sexual arousal. In the case of the dog, for example, the nose of the male is exquisitely sensitive to the odor of a sexual attractant, classified as a pheromone, which is released into the atmosphere from the vagina of a female in heat. It is released only at the time when she is ovulatory, or in heat. From a far distance downwind, males sniff the pheromonal molecules and pursue them to their source. Then ensues a kind of mating doggy dance in which the bitch teasingly alternates invitation and coy retreat, and the assembled male dogs sniff and prance around, sizing up their competitive chances, until the bitch selectively accepts one of them and copulates with him.

Among primates, the eyes predominantly replace the nostrils as the organs of sexual arousal. In some species, hormonally controlled swelling and vivid coloration of the hind parts of the female at mid-cycle attract the male at the time when she is ovulating. The male primate has no corresponding visual display with which to attract the female, except maybe the erection of his penis.

So far as is obviously evident, in females of the human species visible sexual attractivity does not fluctuate in synchrony with the hormonal changes of the menstrual cycle, but exists in a steady state, augmented from time to time by the artifice of dress and cosmetic adornment. Men and women are similar in having a more or less steady state of sexual attractivity and arousability.

Dependence on the eyes for sexuoerotic arousal is sex-shared but threshold-dimorphic. Men have a lower threshold for visual arousal than women do, whereas women have a lower threshold for tactual arousal. This difference applies not only to the visual image as actually perceived, but also as recalled from memory, or inserted into the story line of fantasy and dream. Regardless of whether it is presented pictorially or described verbally, the imagery of commercial pornography for men is predominantly visual, whereas for women it is predominantly tactual and less dependent on explicit depiction of the genitals and their copulatory union.

Flirtation

Among human beings, when strangers meet and are destined to become aroused to courtship and coitus, their arousal is preceded by a little drama of flirtation. The place where they meet may have a reputation as a meeting place. It may be a recreational facility, a health club, a singles bar, a vacation tour ship or resort, a city square or park, or a location known colloquially as a cruising and pickup spot or a meat rack. Being in such a place is a preliminary indication of being prepared for flirtation. Among females, the prevailing role is to be on display, so as to attract the visual attention of the male. Among males, the prevailing role is to be attracted and to make a move. In this reciprocal way, two people establish eye contact.

After eye contact has been established, the little drama of flirtation proceeds as predictably as if regulated by a formula. The sequence of flirtatious maneuvers is the same in cosmopolitan cities (Perper, 1985) as in remote jungle villages of Amazonia and New Guinea (Eibl-Eibesfeldt, 1972). After establishing eye contact, the sign that indicates a two-way interest is mutual holding of the gaze which is reinforced possibly by a tell-tale blush. Next, one of the two people tests the other by demurely drooping the eyelids so as to avert the gaze. This maneuver is a test to see whether, when the gaze is shyly returned with a squint, smile, or flutter of the eyelashes, the other person has continued to look. It is a maneuver that may be repeated during conversation, and as a prelude to moving closer together. The opening gambit in conversation may be as banal as asking what time it is. It is not the content of conversation that counts, but the vocal animation of the dialogue, as though any triviality can be spoken so as to convey the importance of making an impression. As dialogue continues, the flow of speech accelerates with heavier breathing, louder sound, and vocal exaggeration, no matter how insignificant the meaning. The message is in the delivery which includes laughter, even if the humor is contrived. As they talk, the two people, if seated, rotate so that they face one another and bring themselves closer together. The tongue flicks out, moistening the lips. As if for greater comfort, clothing is shed or casually adjusted and fortuitously reveals bare skin, or more of it, around at least the neck, wrists, and ankles. Arm and leg positions are changed and extended in gestures that bring them, as if inadvertently, into contact with the other person. Provided there is no recoil, then closer touching, pressing, patting, or holding ensues. Before they know what they are doing, the two people begin mirroring each the other's gestures and their bodies move in synchrony as if in anticipation of the reciprocal movements of kissing, sexual foreplay, and sexual intercourse.

In addition to what can be captured on a video with sound, there is the accompanying private experience of increased heart rate, rapid breathing, perspiration, and butterflies in the stomach. If the first encounter has as its sequel limerence, or falling in love, then the bodily signs over time may include changes in eating, sleeping, dreaming, fantasizing, concentration, and distractibility, all of which are more severe if flirtation is followed by love that is lopsided or unrequited.

The little drama of flirtation is played also by couples who are not strangers but lovers or spouses. For them the beginning may be accelerated so as to lead sooner into the bodily contact of foreplay and coitus, but to omit flirtation altogether may turn penovaginal intromission into a perfunctory, if not a repulsive performance for both partners, or if not for both, then more likely for the woman than the man.

Academic and Career Achievement

It is possible to speculate that the nine parameters of sex-shared/threshold-dimorphic behavior provide a largely phyletic basis on which educational and vocational male/female differences are developmentally superimposed. To illustrate, it may be speculated that male territorial mapping or marking is the phyletic foundation for a greater affinity for mathematical and related scientific scholarship in boys and men as compared with girls and women. Conversely, it may be speculated that female homemaking and care of the young, which includes talking to their babies and providing them a native language, is the phyletic foundation for a greater affinity for verbal and related humanistic scholarship in girls and women as compared with boys and men.

The justification for both of these speculations is that they try to explain statistically observed data on male/female differences in educational and vocational achievement that no one can deny. One observed difference is that the average male score in tests of mathematical and related scientific scholarship is higher than the average female score. Conversely, the average female score on tests of verbal and related humanistic scholarship is higher than the average male score.

Another observed difference is that from the age of puberty onward, more males than females are in the highest echelon of achievement in mathematical and related scientific scholarship. The converse of this observed difference should be that from puberty onward more females than males are in the highest echelon of achievement in verbal and related humanistic scholarship. But that is not the case. It is more accurate to say that a disproportionate number of females drop out of the competition before reaching the highest echelon of either mathematical or verbal achievement. Yes, there have been women accorded the highest level of achievement in mathematics and its sciences, but on less than a 50:50 basis with men. Women have also been acclaimed at the highest level of literature, arts and humanistic studies, but again on less than a 50:50 basis with men. The reverse applies to men who have since ancient times disproportionately outnumbered women in achieving recognition at the highest level of scholarship and authorship, no matter what their field of specialty in science, humanities, or arts.

Although its foundation may be phyletically determined, the final form of male/female difference in educational and vocational achievement is the product of determinism that is both multivariate and sequential. There is no technology for isolating a phyletic determinant and measuring it. Just as their is no test of the isolated essence of language ability, so also with other phyletic determinants. Similarly, just as language ability can be measured only by inference from the evidence of its performance, so also with the measurement of male/female differences in any educational or vocational abilities. At any age, however, performance of the ability is already the product of multiple variables acting in sequence, and those variables may themselves very directly augment or diminish male/female differences. Variables that augment male/female differences in academic achievement pertain, in part, to educational history.

From the era of Socrates and Plato in fifth century B.C. Athens until the nineteenth century in Europe, academic institutions for males were off limits to females. Apart from studying in convents or with private governesses (for the daughters of the wealthy), females had no educational facilities of their own. Girls could not be competitive with boys, for they did not share the same curriculum. With the advent of universal education and the beginning of coeducational instruction in the nineteenth century, the curriculum for boys was, according to untested medical doctrine of the times, dangerous to the health of girls: medical dogma held that too much expenditure of intellectual energy, especially in combination with depletion of vitality caused by menstruation, would enfeeble the female constitution and diminish the power of procreation.

The stereotype of the division of labor into men's and women's work was carried over into the curriculum of the twentieth-century classroom from kindergarten to college. In professional schools the vested male interest in excluding female competition still dies a lingering death and curtails the possibility of equality of competition and achievement. Boys and girls themselves assimilate and perpetuate the popular platitudes about the disparity between them regarding their prospects in, respectively, mathematics and science versus language and humanities.

These same platitudes have surreptitiously found their way into contemporary research on sex differences in cognitive abilities (Halpern, 1992). The tests on which women have been reported to outperform men are trivial and unprestigious, whereas men outperform women on complex and prestigious ones. The women's tests are: verbal fluency (but not comprehension), perceptual speed (like marking all names containing five letters) and fine manual dexterity (as in fitting pegs into a pegboard). The men's tasks are recognizing rotations of three dimensional shapes on a two dimensional surface, mathematical reasoning, and targeting (not being distracted by competing stimuli).

Various attempts have been made to link the foregoing male/female differences to X and Y chromosomal status, to levels of sex hormones measured in blood or saliva, and to brain laterality. Although the findings are inconsistent and inconclusive, they have led to the oversimplified depiction of the left brain function as predominantly intuitive, socially empathic, agentive, and feminine. By contrast the corresponding oversimplified depiction of right brain function is predominantly logical, visuo-spatial, instrumental, and masculine. Here again the male depiction is more prestigious than that of the female. In the trappings of modern science, these depictions together reincarnate the earlier pejorative stereotype that depreciates the female's intellect and aggrandizes the male's as superior, in support of the erstwhile shibboleth that it is foolish for the female to compete academically and vocationally with the male. Far from being a phyletically determined, this shibboleth of male/female difference is the product of cultural and political overlay. There is hemispheric difference in the way that the brain processes information, the right hemisphere being specialized in recognizing familiar regularities and forms, for example, and the left in recognizing unfamiliar irregularities and distortions (Zaidel, 1994), but this difference applies to both females and males.

Irrespective of their origins, manifest differences between males and females in academic and vocational achievement, and in aspirations as well, do exist today, and on an individual basis they cannot be abolished by edict. They are not universal, however. Some boys are in the girls' league and some girls in the boys' league. For them it would be democratically fair-minded if they encounter no competitive barriers to membership in the highest echelons of all types of achievement, academically, vocationally, and otherwise.

· 3 ·

Four Categories of
Gender Coding

Formulating Principles
Sex Irreducible Gender Coding
Sex Derivative Gender Coding
Sex Adjunctive Gender Coding
Sex Adventitious Gender Coding

· 3 ·

Four Categories of
Gender Coding

Formulating Principles

Among human beings, the context in which phylisms may be expressed is often circumscribed by rules of politeness and other traditional societal constraints. Although they may have great antiquity, these traditions, unlike phylisms themselves, are not universal. Instead they are historically and transculturally variable, at least to some extent. They prescribe a society's customary ways of doing things. They formulate stereotypic roles to which individuals are expected or obliged to conform.

One of the great principles on which stereotypic roles are organized is age. Another is dominance and the distribution of power and authority. A third is sex and the procreative subdivision of the species into males and females. Whereas these three principles are universal and apply to the human species everywhere, the stereotypic roles constructed around them are not. Rather they differ from one another on the basis of different local origins and antecedents. Stereotypic roles have a history of having been constructed arbitrarily and inconsistently rather than logically and systematically. Thus, on the criterion of sex, today's stereotypic roles for males and females are biased toward insufficient attention to the similarities between the sexes and exaggeration of the differences. Such bias is evident in the stereotypic division of labor between men's and women's work roles. This division made sense during most of human history, when life expectancy was as short as thirty or forty years, as it is in many Third World countries today. During most of their short adult lives women were occupied with childbearing and infant rearing, which curtailed their free-ranging mobility, as compared with men. Women's labor was domestic and within range of the campfire. They were guardians of the flame. Men's labor was further afield, hunting for food and guarding against marauders. In modern times, as circumstances have changed, it is feasible to pay increasingly greater attention to the similarities between men and women and what they can do interchangeably. Nonetheless, pregnancy is not interchangeable, nor is breast feeding of infants. These belong to the sex irreducible category of male/female differences. This category is the first of four: sex irreducible, sex derivative, sex adjunctive, and sex adventitious.

Sex Irreducible Gender Coding

Among those who debate the relative merits of males and females in mathematics and science versus verbal scholarship, it comes as a surprise that the only irreducible and nonoverlapping differences between the sexes are confined to procreation, namely that men impregnate and women menstruate, ovulate, gestate, and lactate. There are several species of fish that breed for part of their lives as females, and for part as males (Chan, 1977; Shapiro, 1987), but such a complete degree of sex changing is unknown in mammalian species. There are some human beings, diagnosed as transexuals, who change sex socially, hormonally, surgically, and legally but, much as they may envy sex-changing fish, they are not able to breed in the sex which they adopt.

The surgical technique of organ transplantation that would enable them to do so has not yet been perfected. It is conceivable, however, that advances in molecular biology and gene mapping may make it possible to program the procreative organs into embryological reverse and then into redevelopment as those of the other sex.

For the male-to-female transexual, the possibility of implantation of a donated egg fertilized in vitro with semen from the partner has not yet been realized. Its realization will require perfection of the technique of implanting the fertilized egg into the abdominal cavity and ensuring that a pregnancy will ensue despite the absence of a uterus. Ectopic or extrauterine pregnancies with delivery by laparotomy are not unknown.

There is one renowned case of a New Zealand woman who carried a normal baby girl to term after having had a hysterectomy (Jackson et al., 1980). A freshly fertilized egg had been left behind in the abdominal cavity. It attached itself to the outside wall of the small intestine, grew itself a placenta, and developed from an embryo into a baby.

For the male-to-female transexual, an alternative to extrauterine pregnancy would require the formidable task of overcoming immunorejection of a donated and surgically transplanted uterus. Transplantation of an ovary would not be essential as it is possible for a woman without ovaries to carry a donated, in-vitro-fertilized egg to full term pregnancy in her own uterus. Such a pregnancy does not require that the mother's chromosomal sex be 46, XX, as for a typical female. Donor pregnancies have been carried successfully by mothers who had a history of 46, XY (male) hermaphroditic birth defect (Frydman et al., 1988; Sauer et al., 1989). They lacked ovaries but did have a partially formed uterus which responded to hormonal treatment to regulate pregnancy.

Ordinary men do not lactate, but there are some hormonal anomalies that allow the glandular tissue of the male breast to enlarge and secrete milk. The same effect can be produced experimentally in animals.

Even in times past, a baby's life and death did not hinge on its access to its own mother's breast, for a wet nurse could be employed as a substitute. Today, men as well as women can feed a baby with formula from a bottle, or baby food from a jar. Maternal breast feeding, although the ideal source of nourishment, does not have the same significance as an irreducible male/female difference that it used to have.

From the foregoing, one learns that even the irreducible procreative sex differences are less than absolute when scrutinized under the light of extreme cases.

Sex Derivative Gender Coding

From adolescence onward, the irreducible procreative sex differences are under the governance of sex hormones which influence also behavior that is gender coded as sex derivative. Without testosterone secreted into the blood stream from their own Leydig cells, testicles fail to make sperms in their microtubules. Testosterone is also necessary for the secretion from the prostate gland and seminal vesicles of the fluid in which sperms are ejaculated.

Testicles are stimulated to secrete testosterone by two hormones secreted into the blood stream by the pituitary gland located deep inside the head behind the bridge of the nose. In females, the same two hormones stimulate the ovaries. Since ovaries and testicles share the common name of gonads, the pituitary hormones are known as gonadotropins. One of them is FSH (follicle stimulating hormone). It stimulates the ovarian follicle to secrete estrogen during the first half of each monthly cycle. The other is LH (luteinizing hormone). It stimulates the ovarian follicle, after its ovum has burst in mid-cycle, to secrete progesterone. Progesterone is needed for pregnancy, if the ovum unites with a sperm; and for menstruation, if it does not.

Ever since farmers began castrating farm animals in ancient times, it has been known that loss of the testicles produces not only sterility, but also alters muscle and fat distribution, and produces greater docility. The blood level of male hormone from the testicles falls to that of prepuberty, but the small supply from the adrenocortical glands and possibly from brain cells continues.

A castrated man differs from an uncastrated man in approximately the same way as a prepubertal boy differs from a well-developed adolescent or young man. After castration, the main differences are sterility, diminished genitosexual performance, and weaker subjective feeling of orgasm, and less muscular and more fat tissue without alteration of bone shape and size. Balding is arrested and docility questionably increases.

The term docility is like its opposite, aggressivity, a catchall that needs to be subdivided. Docility subdivides into lessened pursuit of potential sexual partners, reduced mating rivalry, reduced dominance assertion, and reduced athleticism. Docility may reflect a reduction in physical assault consequent on less muscle power and athleticism, but it does not necessarily reflect a lessening of disputatiousness. In former times, the court eunuchs of Muslim potentates and Chinese emperors, as well as the castrati of European opera, were adept in dispute and in devious manipulation of power. In today's medical world, the castration of male-to-female transexuals followed by female hormone treatment is not especially associated with ensuing docility.

The opposite of docility is often postulated to be not simply disputatiousness or aggressivity but abusive violence. The corollary of this postulate is that violence is testosterone driven. It is even claimed that the greater degree of violence, the higher the level of testosterone. However, the evidence for this claim is not robust. Likewise there is a lack of robust evidence for the claim that a high level of testosterone (sometimes referred to caustically as testosterone poisoning) drives men to abuse, rape, and kill women. It is politically correct to equate violence and brutality with masculinity, and docility and victimhood with femininity. Statistics in support of this politically correct proposition are slanted, if not actually deceitful. Although their strategies may be different from those of men, women do assault, maim, and murder their mates, and their children also, despite their low levels of testosterone (Dunn, 1994).

In some present-day cases when a eunuch becomes deprived of or noncompliant in maintaining his supply of replacement testosterone, he may experience unexplained crying spells of sudden onset, and maybe hot flashes also. As in the case of women at the menopause, these symptoms are attributable to rapid reduction in the level of gonadal sex hormones, without a corresponding reduction in the level of gonadotropins.

The converse of depriving males of male hormone is providing females with it. Female-to-male transexualism provides relevant information. The superimposition of a masculinizing puberty on an adult female is more successful than suppression of masculinization in an adult male. The permanent effects of masculinization of the natal female are deepening of the voice, increased distribution of body and facial hair, baldness if there is a genetic predisposition, and slight enlargement of the clitoris. Subcutaneous fat padding decreases and muscular tissue increases, but the bone shape and size remain unchanged. There may be an increase in muscular energy expenditure, although not of conspicuous magnitude, and not paralleled by an increase in aggressivity. Menstruation is suppressed and so is fertility, but both can be restored by withdrawal of male hormone. The frequency of feeling "horny" may increase, and so may the intensity of clitoral feeling and orgasm.

The hormonal feminization of male-to-female transexuals with estrogen, or estrogen plus progesterone, mimics the effects of surgical castration, but on a reversible basis. Female hormone treatment feminizes, but it does not reverse masculinization that has already taken place. Thus it does not demasculinize the voice, nor the beard and body hair, but it does reduce oiliness of the skin and induce breast enlargement, as in a pubescent girl. The ultimate size of the breasts is individually variable. There is much individual variation in the effect of estrogenic or progestinic hormonal treatment on male genitosexual functioning and subjectively experienced eroticism. Overall the effect is that of a sexuoerotic tranquilizer.

In nontransexual females, the loss of ovarian hormones may be by surgical castration (ovariectomy, sometimes superfluously combined with hysterectomy), or by the physiological changes of the menopause.

One outcome is infertility. Another is cessation of the hormonal governance of lactation. The outcome on sexual life is subtle and individually different, but one effect that transcends individual difference is dryness and fragility of the vaginal wall. Estrogen is necessary for vaginal lubrication. When deficient it may be replaced by prescription.

The full extent to which estrogen and progesterone contribute to erotosexual potential and function remains an unsolved question. The answer may be that testosterone, normally present at a low level in the female blood stream, is the so-called libido hormone for women as it is also for men. An alternative possibility, highly speculative, is that estradiol is the so-called libido hormone for both sexes. In men, brain cells that need estradiol could aromatize it from testosterone. In women, estradiol is secreted from the ovaries.

The effect of hormonal deficiency on sensory acuity as a consequence of castration has not been investigated in either women or men. However, the possibility that sensory acuity is hormonally mediated is suggested by not only male/female differences, but also by fluctuations in acuity (notably in olfactory acuity) in synchrony with the hormonal changes of the menstrual cycle (Velle, 1987) in women.

Another difference between males and females that appears to be sex hormone derived, but in ways yet to be fathomed, relates to morbidity and mortality. The life expectancy of women is higher than that of men, regardless of the average length of life. In the United States today, the life expectancy is in the middle to upper eighties for women, and in the seventies for men. From infancy onward, the death rate is higher for males than for females. Even before birth, fetal wastage is greater for male than female fetuses. As if in preparation for losses that lie ahead, the birth rate is higher for boys than girls, typically 105:100. It is more hazardous to be a male than a female, regardless of the causes of death, except for autoimmune diseases and diseases of the female reproductive system.

From the foregoing sex hormone dependent differences between males and females, two differences stand out in particular. One is physique, which includes bone structure and muscularity. The male, on the average, is greater in size and brute strength than is the female. The other is mammary anatomy and function. Only the female is equipped to nourish the newborn and young infant without artificial aid. Historically, and up to the present, these two differences are typical of those upon which sex adjunctive gender coding has been superimposed.

Sex Adjunctive Gender Coding

Developmentally in prenatal and earliest neonatal life, sex hormonalization of the brain leaves a lasting imprint that eventually will exert an influence on postpubertal hormonal functioning and correspondingly on gender coded behavior of the type classified as sex derivative. This, in turn, will exert its own influence on gender coding classified as sex adjunctive. To reiterate a prime example: fetal and neonatal brain hormonalization exerts an influence subsequently on the hormonal governance of fertility, lactation, and breast feeding, which in turn restricts the geographical range of women's mobility, which in turn increases the range of women's on-site domestic and residential activities that become gender stereotyped as women's work.

Historically and transculturally, women's work has included growing food in gardens; gathering plant and animal foods; raising yard animals and birds for food; preparing and cooking food for dependents, including men; carrying fuel and water; weaving and sewing clothing; making pottery, baskets, and household utensils; being midwives, and so on.

The gender coding of labor on the criterion of distance from the home base ignores the criterion of physique and muscle power. Hard labor is gender coded for women as well as men. Men do, however, have more size and muscular strength on average than women do, and their hard labor is compatible with their being distant and long absent from those who remain near the home base. Men may be away hunting, seafaring, trading, marauding, warring, exploring, prospecting, or engaging in industrial or commercial activity.

Prehistoric travel by foot eventually gave way to travel in boats, on the backs of domesticated animals, and in wheeled vehicles hauled by animals. Wheeled travel was so strongly gender coded for men that when in recent times automotive steam and internal combustion engines replaced horses, building, driving, and repairing the engines became gender coded as men's work—and likewise for airplane and rocket engines. Although that code has been broken somewhat, in most countries of the world the work of engineers and mechanics is still predominantly men's work. Driving commercial trucks and buses, like sailing ships and piloting airplanes, may also be coded as masculine. In ultraconservative and fundamentalist Islamic cultures, even the driving of a private automobile is gender coded as masculine. In such a culture for a woman to be unescorted is prima facie evidence of her being available for adultery or prostitution. Therefore only men are licensed to drive.

The long chain of descent from hormones to physique and from long distance travel by foot to riding horses, captaining boats, driving locomotives and automobiles, piloting planes and rockets, or having expertise in engineering and mechanics, is gender coded as masculine all the way. Masculine gender coding extends adjunctively to the pursuit of mathematics and physical and engineering sciences educationally and occupationally.

The gender stereotyping of mathematics and physical and engineering sciences as men's work may have additional roots also in the phylism of boundary marking which is stronger, on average in males than females (see also chap. 2). In subprimates it is testosterone derived and olfactory. In primates it is visual. In the human intellect it may translate into recognition of directionality, mapping of spatial configurations and three-dimensional shapes, and calculation of distances, all of which, in turn, may translate into the social evolution of mathematics and science, and to their gender coding as masculine occupations, as has been the case in our own cultural history.

Some but not all societies have traditionally coded weaving, sewing, basketry, and pottery making as feminine. All of these occupations entail the application of design. They also are intellectually dependent on directionality, mapping, and calculation which in turn translate into the gender coding of mathematics and science as feminine occupations, despite contemporary gender stereotyping to the contrary. It is the occupational stereotyping that is gender dimorphic, not the fundamental mental functioning of those who are stereotyped.

The counterpart of this logic applies to scholarship and careers for men in the humanities and social studies. It is widely held on the basis of contemporary educational testing that, whereas boys on the average outclass girls in mathematics and physical sciences, girls outclass boys in literature and social studies. Nonetheless, prestige careers in literature, humanities, and the arts, have for centuries and until very recently been the prerogative of men. Gender stereotyping of prestige careers of all types as masculine has been a defining characteristic of Western civilization for centuries. Thus even though the domestic career of cook is coded feminine, renamed as the career of chef in a hotel or restaurant, it is gender coded as masculine.

Exceptions and inconsistencies notwithstanding, sex adjunctive gender coding of labor is worldwide. It is transmitted to the young as a gender-coded curriculum in both formal and informal education. It is incorporated into the doctrines and ceremonies of religion and so accrues the prestige, authority, and status of an eternal verity ordained by the Almighty and attributed to His natural law. In the twentieth century, however, in the wake of the feminist movement and of the advance of the automation and computerization of labor, the work roles of men and women have become increasingly interchangeable.

It may be taken as a general rule that all change threatens. Conservative segments of the population are threatened by gender uncoding of the sex adjunctive division of labor and they resist it, sometimes vehemently, as being against God's law. Similarly, in the seventies, they resisted the change from short to long haircuts for males. For them the gender uncoding of labor, like haircuts, is equivalent to the forfeiture of masculinity or femininity in its entirety, as in a transexual's change of sex. Their apprehension is unfounded. Provided boys and girls grow up with uncompromised pride in their genital organs and in the prospect of their future erotic and procreative use, any kind of work is compatible with their masculinity or femininity.

Unisex gender coding of sex adjunctive educational, and occupational roles does not spill over into sexuoerotic roles and does not change the sex of the partner with whom one falls in love. It does not change heterosexuality into homosexuality or bisexuality. If there is a social illusion to the contrary, then it stems from the error of reversing cause and effect when trying to account for the presence of homosexual men and women in occupations formerly coded, respectively, for females and males only.

The phenomenon of men in women's occupations and women in men's occupations has an ancient history and wide distribution across cultures. In a society that has strict occupational gender coding, those who gravitate toward being gender transposed occupationally do so on the basis of having a predisposition toward such a career, insofar as they have grown up to be sufficiently transposed in gender identity within themselves. Occupational and educational gender crossing is something they assimilate and identify with from early childhood. In childhood the antecedents of occupational gender crossing in adulthood may be manifested in play that rehearses the occupations of adulthood. Thus, some gender-transposed boys will delight in theatrical impersonation, in designing clothing or interiors for women, or in styling women's hair. Correspondingly, some gender-transposed girls will delight in being a stablehand, a guerilla terrorist, or an airline pilot, and so on.

Occupational rehearsal play is a prominent feature of childhood recreation. In addition, some of the gender-coded play of childhood becomes professionalized into gender-coded careers of adulthood—for example, professional fighting and professional big league sports that are symbolic battles. Childhood playacting itself and other expressions of the arts also may be developmental preparations for careers in adulthood that are gender-coded. Wherever theatrical tradition excludes women from the stage, men must be cast to act female roles, which creates the paradox that a man's career is to impersonate a woman. Female impersonation is an ideal vocation for those, such as effeminate male homosexuals, for example, who have a childhood history of a proclivity for role taking, particularly if their proclivity is to take the role of a female.

Occupational, educational, and recreational gender coding carry with them not only the force of custom and weight of religion, but also the power of the law. The law distributes power between the sexes inequitably, and it penalizes those who do not conform to its edicts of gender coding, particularly with respect to the use of the sex organs. The power of the law is the link between sex adjunctive and sex adventitious gender coding (Money, 1988a, pp. 68–69).

Sex Adventitious Gender Coding

The fourth grade of gender coding, classified as sex adventitious, is the one that is at the farthest remove from sex irreducible coding and that has the least connection with sex hormones. Sex adventitious gender coding does, however, pay attention to hormone related male/female differences either by amplifying and exaggerating them, or less frequently by neglecting or trivializing them. Either way, there is a high degree of arbitrariness and variability in place and time with respect to the inventory of what is included.

The inventory of phenomena that are adventitiously gender coded covers the full range of human enterprise and activity and is subdivisible under the following rubrics: apparel, adornment, body language, vocal language, etiquette, recreation, education, vocation, and legal rights.

Unobtrusively infused into all the manifestations of adventitious feminine gender coding is a principle that may be named the vulnerability principle. It signifies that, in Western if not all cultures, adventitious feminine gender coding is based on the proposition that the female is vulnerable, weak, and dependent for protection on the superiority, strength, and power of the male. A second principle may be named the allurative principle to signify that adventitious feminine gender coding is based on a second proposition, namely, that the female is an alluring and cosseted showpiece for male aggrandizement by displaying the male's wealth and romantic prowess.

The reciprocal of each of these principles applies to adventitious masculine gender coding. Thus, the reciprocal of the vulnerability principle is the expendability principle according to which men are expendable, fearless, and aggressive. The reciprocal of the allurative principle is the solicitational principle, namely that the man has the power of wealth and property with which to solicit the female.

Adventitiously gender-coded roles are perpetuated as stereotypes of masculinity and femininity. Their arbitrariness makes them logical targets for the attack of social constructionists, and lends superficial credence to their theory that all gender-coded roles are the product exclusively of arbitrary social constructs.

The perpetuation of arbitrarily gender-coded roles is guaranteed not only by habit and custom, but also by the degree to which they are written into law. Hence the historical importance of legislation that has reconstructed the law so as to give women the right to vote, for instance, and to ensure equal educational and vocational opportunity for males and females.

Where the wearing of uniforms is mandatory, as in some schools and various uniformed services, if clothing is not gender coded, then males and females are likely to be distinguishable by hair style and cosmetics. Gender coding in matters of apparel, personal adornment, and hairstyle is dictated for the most part by fashion and its changes, whereas changes in the gender coding of etiquette, manners, and morals as well as of body language and vocal language are more likely to be by slow drift than by abrupt fashion change. In the electronic age of television and videos, new trends spread rapidly and over long distances, world wide.

· 4 ·

Feminism before and after Gender

Woman's Suffrage
Female Sexology: Nineteenth Century
Penicillin and the Pill
Neutering of Gender
Sexualization of Oppression

· 4 ·

Feminism before and
after Gender

Woman's Suffrage

The history of the institution of arranged marriage goes hand in hand
with the history of hierarchical preservation of power, privilege, and
wealth in a class-stratified society. Both are extremely ancient, and in
both the maximum of power, privilege, and wealth is gender-coded as
male. Historically, the father, in arranging the marriage of his offspring,
transferred his authority over his daughter to her husband. Made sacred
by the authority of the Bible, the authority of the male over the female
spread wherever the Bible spread and, if indigenous customs were more
egalitarian, displaced them. Under the laws of medieval feudalism every woman became a satellite of her husband. She had no property rights,
no right to her own earnings, no educational or vocational rights, no judicial rights, and no right to political enfranchisement so as to correct
these wrongs. They remained uncorrected even as late as the colonial
period of America.

The modern feminist movement for women's rights might be said
to have begun with "A Vindication of the Rights of Woman," an essay
published in 1792 by Mary Wollstonecraft, wife of the social reformer
William Godwin and mother of Mary Wollstonecraft Shelley, author of
Frankenstein and second wife of the poet Percy Bysshe Shelley.

Mary Wollstonecraft petitioned her readers to "let us consider women in the grand light of human creatures who in common with men are pleased on this earth to unfold their faculties," and to permit women to be represented in Parliament. Progress would need to be made synchronously on three fronts. The right to political enfranchisement would be costly, and so the right to own property and wealth would be essential, which in turn would require the right to education and training for all professions and occupations.

In England the first women's suffrage committee was formed in 1865 in Manchester. The corresponding event in the United States was an attempt made in Kansas in 1867 at the close of the Civil War to link the franchise for women with that for newly emancipated male slaves, unsuccessfully for both. This was not, however, the beginning of the women's suffrage movement in America. In 1848, the regional Yearly Meeting of the Society of Friends (Quakers) announced the first women's rights convention, which was begun without delay at the home of Mrs. Elizabeth Cady Stanton in Seneca Falls, New York, and continued in Rochester.

The women's suffrage movement met with extraordinary and all-too-often irrational resistance, worldwide. Success was first achieved in New Zealand in 1893, but not until 1918 in Britain and Canada, in 1920 in the United States by way of the Nineteenth Amendment to the Constitution, and in other countries much later or not at all.

The right to vote, although it dominated the agenda of the women's rights movement of the nineteenth and early twentieth century, was not the only item on the agenda of overall reform affecting women. Another item on the American agenda was the reform of women's apparel. In accordance with the principles of nineteenth-century health reform (the equivalent of twentieth-century holistic medicine), the principle of apparel reform was loose-fitting styles for women instead of wasp-waisted, tightly constricting whale-boned corsets. The reform style was a kind of pants suit with a loose tunic and baggy trousers either plain or gathered and frilly around the ankles. The gathered type became eponymically named bloomers, after Amelia Jenks Bloomer, prominent in the temperance and suffrage movements. Bloomers became an emblem of women's rights, and a uniform worn by suffragist demonstrators. Opponents were able to use them as a source of ridicule which surreptitiously raised eyebrows about women's conjugal sexual rights, a topic that dare not be broached openly in public, nor in private, for that matter.

Nonetheless, women's conjugal sexual rights, no matter how un-speakable, were of major importance. This was the era, before germ theory came on the scene in 1870, when women in childbirth died by the thousands from infectious puerperal fever transmitted by the very doctors who delivered their babies, and who ignored the warnings of the Hungarian obstetrician, Ignaz Philipp Semmelweiss, and his statistical demonstration of the physician's role in transmitting the infection. Women of the poverty class died also from a lack of resistance to other diseases brought on by excessive frequency of pregnancy. Abortion was dangerous and illicit. Teachings about the safe period placed it at mid-cycle and were wrong by a full 180 degrees (Trall, 1881/1974). The mass production and marketing of condoms had followed industrial discoveries for the vulcanization of rubber by Goodyear in America in 1839 and Hancock in England in 1840. Like other forms of birth control, condoms were crude and not wholly reliable. In America, Anthony Comstock's fanatically antisexual laws of 1873 made it a criminal offense to advertise, supply, or transmit any information about birth control.

Female Sexology: Nineteenth Century

Medical sexology in the nineteenth century was still dominated by Tissot's eighteenth-century theory of degeneracy brought on by semen wastage. Simon André Tissot's treatise was first published in Latin in 1758. It went through many French and British editions prior to the first American edition (1832/1974) translated as: *A Treatise on the Diseases Produced by Onanism.*

Although he wrote about the "social vice," Tissot was in his *Treatise* in search of a way to control the epidemic of the "social disease" which, after the advent of germ theory in the 1870s, would be subdivided into syphilis and gonorrhea. The theory of semen depletion, found in ancient Chinese medical teaching of the yin and yang principles; and in Ayurvedic medical texts and oral traditions dating back two and a half thousand years and more, became the cornerstone of Tissot's *Treatise.* In Ayurvedic teaching, semen is the most concentrated and powerful source of *sukra*, the vital spirit, and its depletion is a source of illness and eventual death.

Tissot correctly recognized the symptoms of syphilis and gonorrhea alone or in combination. He correctly associated them with promiscuity in the patronage and performance of prostitution, and with the affected offspring of prostitutes and other women whom their male customers infected. His colossal intellectual error was to equate the loss of semen in promiscuity with prostitutes with its loss in masturbation. This error released a two-hundred-year cascade of medical, moral, and religious antisexual mania. Masturbation was the chief culprit, but conjugal depletion of semen was an offender too. The conjugal ideal was that sexual intercourse should be performed infrequently and only for procreation, not for pleasure.

By not having semen, women were viewed as having less vital spirit and less physical and mental energy than men. It was necessary for a wife to conserve not only her own quota of vital spirit, but to be the guardian of her husband's supply also by not consenting to sexual intercourse too often. This was her duty irrespective of her own enjoyment and orgasmic capability, according to the long lost and recently found interview data of Clelia Mosher (Mahood and Wenburg, 1980).

The self-appointed expert on the sexology of the Victorian woman was William Acton, a British surgeon known as an authority on venereal disease, prostitution, chastity, and masturbation, as well as honeybee copulation. He wrote in 1857 and in six later editions of his book until 1875, as follows.

> I have taken pains to obtain and compare abundant evidence on this subject, and the result of my inquiries I may briefly epitomize as follows: I should say that the majority of women, happily for them [and for society, says the 5th edition] are not very much troubled with sexual feeling of any kind. What men are habitually, women are only exceptionally. I admit, of course, the existence of sexual excitement, terminating even in nymphomania, a form of insanity that those accustomed to visit lunatic asylums must be fully conversant with; but, with these sad exceptions, there can be no doubt that sexual feeling in the female is, in the majority of cases, in abeyance, and that it requires positive and considerable excitement to be roused at all; and even if roused, which in many instances it never can be, is very moderate compared with that of the male. Many men, and particularly young men, form their ideas of women's feelings from what they notice early in life among loose, or at least low and vulgar women. There is always a certain number of females who, though not ostensibly prostitutes, make a kind of trade of a pretty face. They are fond of admiration; they like to attract attention of those immediately around them. Any susceptible boy is easily led to believe, whether he is altogether overcome by the siren or not, that she, and hence all women, must have at least as strong passions as himself. Such women, however, give a very false idea of the condition of sexual feeling in general. Association with the loose women of London streets, in casinos and other

immoral haunts, who, if they have not sexual feeling, counterfeit it so well that the novice does not suspect but that it is genuine, all seem to corroborate such an impression. Married men, medical men, or married women themselves, would, if appealed to, tell a different tale, and vindicate female nature from the vile aspersions cast on it by the abandoned conduct and ungoverned lust of a few of its worst examples. There are many females who never feel any excitement whatever. Others, again, immediately after each period, do become, to a limited degree, capable of experiencing it; but this capacity is only temporary, and will cease entirely until the next menstrual period. The best mothers, wives, and managers of households know little or nothing of sexual indulgences. Love of home, of children, of domestic duties, are the only passions they feel. As a general rule, a modest woman seldom desires any sexual gratification for herself. She submits to her husband, but only to please him; and but for the desire of maternity, would far rather be relieved from his attention [pp. 473–474].

Victorian sexological dogma met with strong approval in many home-doctor books, and books of sex and marriage hygiene written by doctors and endorsed by preachers. One extremely influential author in the latter part of the nineteenth century was John Harvey Kellogg, M.D., a great admirer of William Acton. He was fanatical about semen conservation and the reduction of carnal desire which he attributed to a carnivorous diet. To avoid meat on the menu of his Battle Creek Sanitarium, he substituted nut and cereal products. He developed and marketed breakfast cereals, including Kellogg's corn flakes, as lust suppressants and masturbation preventatives.

The voice of antisexualism survived with vehemence into the twentieth century. One of its prestigious exponents was the famed Howard A. Kelly, M.D., founding professor of gynecology at the then new Johns Hopkins University School of Medicine. The *Journal of the American Medical Association* (*JAMA*) had rejected a very enlightened and scientifically explicit article on female sexuality read in 1899 by Denslow Lewis, M.D., a professor of gynecology in Chicago. In the debate that followed in the American Medical Association (AMA), Kelly went on written record in 1900 as follows:

I do not believe pleasure in the sexual act has any particular bearing on the happiness of life; that is the lowest possible view of happiness in married life, and I shall never forget the utter disgust which I felt once when a professional friend of mine in Philadelphia told me that he had repaired the perineum of a mistress for the sake of increasing sexual gratification of her paramour. I do hope we shall not have to go into details in discussing this subject; it is not necessary.

Its discussion is attended with more or less filth and we besmirch ourselves by discussing it in public [quoted in Money, 1985a].

Lewis defended a woman's right to undiluted sexual lust and orgasm. Three years earlier (1896), Alice B. Stockham, M.D., had idealized a more quiescent form of prolonged, nonorgasmic genital union which she named karezza (from the same root as caress). It was a new name for an ancient tantric practice; and also for what John Humphrey Noyes (1872) had named male continence. Noyes was leader of the Oneida Community in upstate New York, known for its practice of group marriage. For Victorian ladies, karezza combined the "exquisite exaltation" of genteel sex with the bonus of birth control provided it was augmented, in case of necessity, by coitus interruptus, should the male reach the point of ejaculatory inevitability.

Even though karezza had few adherents, it nonetheless carried the same message as did the defeat of Lewis in his AMA debate with Kelly and others, namely, that the women's movement must put aside whatever unabashed demands women might have for sexual rights, so that sexual rights would not confound and contaminate the demand for voting rights. Otherwise suffragists would have Acton's "vile aspersions" cast upon them as loose women and harlots. To gain the vote, women were obliged to deprive themselves of the fulsomeness of their sexuality, at least insofar as their public utterances were concerned. A century later, the tables would be turned. Sexuality would again come under attack, but it would be masculine sexuality that was predominantly offensive.

Penicillin and the Pill

The passage of the Nineteenth Amendment in 1920 gave American women the right to vote, but it did not equalize the right to own property, nor to have an extradomestic career with an earned income. It also did not rescind the taboo on the right to contraception and birth control which became the dominant issue, along with sex education, of the sex reform movement in both America and Europe in the first half of the twentieth century. Opposition was intense. In America, the last legal barriers to the universal availability of family planning and contraception were not removed until the 1960s.

The 1930s were the decade of the Great Depression in which the right to work overshadowed all other rights for both sexes. Then followed mobilization for World War II and, in the later forties, the right to recover from the disruptions of war. The postwar baby boom kept women focused on family life, and changed the age ratio of the population. Other issues of women's rights were on hold. Women as well as men became ever more prosperous in the postwar fifties.

It is proverbially true of emancipation that the closer it approaches, the greater the effort to reach it. The advance of the civil rights movement of the 1960s in America is an example, and likewise the onset of the gay rights movement, the revival of the women's movement renamed as the feminist movement, and the spread of the so-called sexual revolution. They all grew rapidly in the decade of the sixties, the decade of resistance to the war in Vietnam.

Unlike the other emancipatory movements, the sexual revolution had no formal organization or governance. Rather, it was an extensively diffused emancipation from the code that restricted personal sexual and erotic encounters and conduct. Chronologically it was preceded by the serendipitous scientific discovery of the first antibiotic, penicillin, and of its efficacy in killing the bacteria of syphilis and gonorrhea. By the end of the forties, penicillin was mass produced and mass marketed for the cure of syphilis and gonorrhea and for the prevention of their epidemic spread (Sheehan, 1982).

Another technological advance of the 1940s was the application of new knowledge of the chemical structure of the sex hormones to allow for pharmaceutical synthesis and mass marketing. With synthetic estrogen and progesterone available in quantity, it became possible to test their contraceptive efficacy at first in animals and then in human clinical trials. The upshot of this endeavor was the contraceptive Pill, first marketed in 1960 (Pincus, 1965; Halberstam, 1993).

Preceding the Pill, the contraceptive diaphragm, as compared with the condom for men, had enabled women to regulate their reproductive timetable themselves, without reliance on the male partner. The Pill had the added advantage of being as discreet as any other tablet, and of being put in the mouth, not the vagina. Moreover, the act of taking it was independent of the timing of the next occasion of sexual intercourse. As well as being safe and effective, it did not signify a specific occasion of coital intent, and did not interrupt the spontaneity of erotic activity.

Men as well as women were emancipated from the dread of the two most dangerous sexually transmitted diseases by penicillin (HIV/AIDS had not yet been identified), and from the educational and vocational disruptions of untimely pregnancy by the Pill. For women whom the Pill affected adversely, the intrauterine device (IUD) was soon introduced as an alternative.

On the basis of logic alone, one might have expected that sexual emancipation and women's emancipation would have proceeded hand in hand in the decade of the sixties; but they did so only to a limited extent. The second wave of the women's movement focused its agenda on equality of educational and vocational opportunity and of earned income, more than on sex and family life. In fact, with the knowledge of hindsight, it can be argued that there was insufficient emphasis on equality in the kitchen. The outcome was that feminist gains in the market place were not accompanied by corresponding gains in shared parenthood and running a household. Either as a single parent, or with a man, a woman who earned an independent income carried the responsibilities of two careers, one inside and one outside the home.

Neutering of Gender

The second wave of the women's movement has belonged primarily to the children of wealth, not those of poverty. It was renamed the feminist movement. Its launching may be attributed to the publication in 1963 of Betty Friedan's book, *The Feminine Mystique*. "I wanted to prove that education was good for women," Friedan explained to *Newsweek* in 1994, "and that it hadn't made them frustrated as wives, mothers, and homemakers. But . . . I found that many were restive and unfulfilled in their traditional roles. 'I'm B.J.'s wife; I'm Jenny's mother,' one woman said, 'but who am I?' I wrote an article on [my] questionnaire results, but nobody ran it. One magazine even wrote to my agent saying, 'Only the most neurotic housewives would identify with this.' The more people I interviewed, the further I saw that this was the problem that has no name."

With the battle for women's voting rights already won in 1920, the feminist movement in America of the sixties focused on the Equal Rights Amendment to the Constitution of the United States which would guarantee equality of legal and civil rights to women as in property ownership, marriage, career, earned income, and suchlike. Equality meant equality with men, which might be stated as equality irrespective of sex; but it could not be stated as sexual equality or equal sexual rights without the lexical dilemma of implicating the other meaning of sex as genital and erotic lust and procreation. The lexical solution to this dilemma was the term *gender* as newly adopted into the vernacular to apply to human beings. In political discourse, *equal rights* came to signify equal rights on the criterion of gender, devoid of genital and procreative sex, eroticism and lust.

For political purposes, gender was shorn of its connection with the genital organs and their activity in lust. In the campaign for the Equal Rights Amendment, people might as well have been Ken and Barbie dolls, as already mentioned in the introduction, with nothing between their legs. Gender was sex neutered and purified so as to be devoid of lust. With the neutering of sex, there is no procreation. In this way the significance of childbearing in women's lives was circumvented in the rhetoric of the feminist movement.

Although the 1950s have become retrospectively idealized as a golden age, they were also the years of McCarthyism and much else that sparked the embers of discontent to become the flames of the liberation movements of the sixties. Overseas, liberation from the oppression of colonial rule set the stage in the United States for the civil rights movement and the liberation of blacks from the oppression of whites which, in turn, provided a model for the women's movement and the liberation of woman from the oppression of male patriarchal power, which in turn was borrowed by the gay rights movement for the liberation of homosexual men and women (soon to be self-identified as gays and lesbians, respectively) from homophobic social and legal discrimination. Gay liberation became a movement for political and civil rights as much as for the right to express one's sexuality and eroticality.

The sexual liberation movement endorsed the right of sexual and erotic expression for all, not only for the heterosexual majority. It was not explicitly a liberation movement for the political and legal rights of sexual nonconformists, but it was in its early days assimilated into the antimilitary and antiestablishment idealism of the countercultural hippie movement of the sixties. Eventually sexual liberation spread more widely to encompass those whose agenda was simply to be liberated from the excessive restrictions imposed by a narrowly moralistic society on the range of permissible sexual and erotic expression.

The various liberation movements differed in the formality and divisions of their corporate structures and in the amount of overlap in their agendas. The feminist movement divided on the issues of gender with and without the inclusion of sexuality. The gender-only faction concentrated on legal and political reform which eventually became the campaign for the Equal Rights Amendment.

Sexualization of Oppression

Sexuality made its first appearance in the feminist movement as a borrowing from the sexual liberation movement. For example, Kate Millet wrote in her book, *Sexual Politics* (1969) that:

> A sexual revolution would require an end of traditional sexual in-
> hibitions and taboos, particularly those that most threaten patri-
> archal monogamous marriage: homosexuality, illegitimacy, and
> adolescent, premarital and extramarital sexuality. The negative aura
> with which sexual activities have generally been surrounded would
> necessarily be eliminated, together with the double standard and
> prostitution. The goal of revolution would be a permissive single
> standard of sexual freedom.

As it gained momentum in the 1970s, the feminist movement, although patterned after other liberation movements, had no explicitly
identified equivalent of colonial oppressors, except that, as in Kate
Millet's statement, oppression of women was attributed generically to
institutionalized patriarchical domination. Then a change took place.
Oppression became explicitly sexualized. Male domination was equated
with male lust. The change was epitomized in Susan Brownmiller's (1975)
book, *Against Our Will*, which paved the way for the *reductio ad
absurdum* in which Andrea Dworkin equated all acts of sexual intercourse with acts of rape. "Violence is male;" she wrote, "the male is the
penis; violence is the penis" (Dworkin, 1979/1989). The same author also
wrote: "By thrusting into her, [the male] takes her over. His thrusting
into her is taken to be her capitulation to him as conqueror; it is a physical surrender of herself to him; he occupies and rules her, expresses his
elemental dominance over her, by his possession of her in the fuck"
(Dworkin, 1987, p. 63).

Radical extremism of the Dworkin type may have appealed to the
sensation-hungry media and to a small faction of the man-hating luna-
tic fringe, but not to feminists who bore no grudge against men, nor to
the men with whom they pairbonded. Ordinary people responded not
to the rhetoric of metaphorical rape, but to its counterpart, the rhetoric
of criminal rape.

In radical feminism, rape was radically redefined, as if by fiat, as
being not an act of sexual assault or coercion, but an act of male violence and aggression perpetrated against women. Demands for increased
legal sanctions against not only stranger rapes, but against also the newly
decreed offenses of date rape and marital rape were met by new legislation. The feminist movement had given its opponents—women like
Phyllis Schlafly and her Eagle Forum, as well as male archconservatives
like Jerry Falwell and his Moral Majority—the first inch of the mile they
would need to defend the continuance of the tradition that woman, the
weaker sex, is dependent on man's power of protection. Woman's role was
surreptitiously being reiterated as the role of martyrdom, and of being

helpless victims of the men who sacrificed them, incompetent to fend for themselves.

The next inch of a return to martyrdom was ceded in 1979 by Women Against Pornography, a subgroup from within the ranks of radical feminism. Their organization could have been extremely naive in not knowing that the full range and role of visual imagery in normal men's erotic arousal is not a replica of what is depicted in commercial pornography, and that much of what is depicted is designed to appeal to a sexually deviant audience (see chap.8). Alternatively, Women Against Pornography, an organization that is conspicuously silent on what constitutes women's pornography, could have been deliberately duped by antifeminist undercover agents assigned to mislead them into attacking all masculine sexual lust. The positive policy would have been to promote the improvement of the products of the pornography industry for female as well as male audiences. The diverse types of imagery of men's commercial pornography are targeted at specific subgroups to which they appeal, like gays, for example, or transvestites. Pornography has many components, not all of which are universal in masculine appeal. Pornography of the type that has erotic appeal to the majority of men (or women) does not convert ordinary decent men into beasts who are dangerous to women.

The truth is that commercial pornography caters not to a random sample of ordinary people, but to specific clienteles comprised of those who have one or another specific bias as to what is erotically arousing. The largest clientele is biased toward specific sexual practices, like oral sex and completely naked display, that are not deviant but are not engaged in at home perhaps for religious, moral, or phobic reasons. Other smaller clienteles are separately biased toward one of the kinky (paraphilic or perverted) sexual scenarios that are an unacceptable turn-off to the partner at home, as well as to the majority of people.

Women Against Pornography failed to allow for the fact that, with no competition from big budget filmmakers, commercial pornography seldom invests in the costly business of dramatically depicting genuine lovers, long-term relationships, authentic erotic ecstasy, and unfaked female orgasms. Instead, it does invest in low budget, short-encounter sex which commonly depicts sexual scenarios of the uninhibited type that might not be performed at home but only with a paid partner, without romantic build-up and without preliminary love play.

The imagery of commercial pornography that is paraphilically kinky or deviant appeals only to a constituency of people who have the same paraphilia. Sadism and masochism (S/M) are examples. Depictions of S/M leave non-S/M people cold. S/M, like all paraphilic sex, is not contagious. It cannot be caught from pictures or videos. S/M pornography does not incite non-S/M viewers into becoming sexual monsters.

Radical feminism is wrong in asserting that commercial pornography teaches males to denigrate women, to use them as sex-objects, and to eroticize their power over women. That is putting the cart before the horse. If men have, since boyhood, been conditioned to denigrate, objectify, or sexually abuse women (or to be abused by them), then they will be attracted to pornography that does the same—otherwise, not.

Women Against Pornography made a great tactical blunder in forming an alliance with the religiously political New Right, as represented at the time by Jerry Falwell's Moral Majority and subsequently by Pat Robertson's Christian Coalition. This alliance was the equivalent of hauling the wooden horse of Troy into the citadel, filled this time with antifeminist fanatics only too eager to fight feminism with the weapon of antipornography. Women, they said, were morally too delicate to be exposed to men's pornography; they needed masculine power and authority to protect them from its evils, which the New Right, in collaboration with governmental policy and judicial censorship, would all too willingly provide.

At the same time as the New Right conspired to undermine sexual liberation and freedom from censorship of sexual expression, it conspired also to help halt women's liberation and to bring about the eventual defeat of the Equal Rights Amendment on June 30, 1982.

· 5 ·

Sexual Counterreformation

Crusade
Abuse and Deprivation in Childhood
Victimology
Freud's Early Seduction Theory Recycled

· 5 ·

Sexual Counterreformation

Crusade

One of the lessons of history is that revolution is followed by counterrevolution, and reformation by counterreformation. Thus the post-World War II years from the late 1940s up to 1960 were characterized by Betty Friedan (1963, pp. 327, 377) as an era of sexual counterrevolution against the revolution that, after 1920 when women gained the right to vote, coincided with the jazz age of the 1920s, the years of the Great Depression of the 1930s, and the World War II years of the 1940s when women were coopted into the workforce. Another counterrevolution, more accurately named a counterreformation, may be said to have followed the sexual revolution of the 1960s and early 1970s. After gearing up in the late 1970s (Money, 1980), the counterreformation accelerated throughout the 1980s, and still, in the mid 1990s, shows no signs of the onset of exhaustion.

The counterreformation did not declare itself by name. If it had a formal organizational structure, it was clandestine. Nonetheless it appears to have been orchestrated rather than to have been haphazard, although the history of its orchestration in government, administration, and religion, and of its covert penetration into community politics and the media has yet to be ascertained. Its first big strategy against sexual liberation was a media campaign in the late seventies against the hazards of an ancient sexually transmitted disease, genital herpes. This campaign was serendipitously reinforced by the discovery in 1981 of the symptoms of a new and lethal sexually transmitted viral disease, HIV/AIDS, which as of the beginning of 1995, is the leading cause of death in both men and women between the ages of 25 and 44.

During the eighties, the counterreformation penetrated the feminist movement, and eventually produced a schism on the issue of pornography (see chaps. 4 and 8), with the antipornography faction continuing to be known as Women Against Pornography, and the propornography faction known as Feminists for Free Expression (Pally, 1994). The counterreformationist attack on pornography went far beyond the confines of feminism into the archconservative organizations of the fundamentalist new right. Thus the report of the Meese Commission (Attorney General's Commission, 1986) completely overturned the report of the earlier Commission on Obscenity and Pornography (1970). Politics indeed makes strange bedfellows! It is strange, indeed, that radical feminism and the phallocentric, patriarchal new right would bed together on the issue of male carnality as manifested in visual pornography. For the new right, pornography exemplified the threat that sexual liberation poses to their moral ideology. For feminism, pornography represented the degradation of women as the objects of phallocentric sexual power and brutality (MacKinnon, 1987; 1993). Neither group recognizes a distinction between pornography that depicts normal sexuality and is erotically arousing to viewers with normal "lovemaps" (Money, 1988b), and pornography that depicts the pathological sexuality of a paraphilia and is erotically arousing only to those whose "lovemap" is correspondingly paraphilic. As already mentioned in chapter 4, sadomasochism is an example. In addition, neither side recognizes that, in the human species, erotic arousal in the male is dependent predominantly on the eyes, whereas in the female the skin senses predominate. This difference accounts for much male/female misunderstanding as, for example, when some mothers go berserk when they find a stash of *Playboy* centerfolds under their teen-age son's mattress, for use as masturbation pictures.

The counterreformation has had various targets other than pornography. There has been insufficient political and public support for a direct attack on premarital and extramarital sex in general, except by way of platitudes on family values and chastity with the futile principle of abstinence ("Just say no") as its slogan. The direct attack on nonmarital sex is covertly racist and is targeted overtly at teen-age pregnancy, which has become characterized as an epidemic of unwed motherhood. The provision of contraception for teen-agers to prevent pregnancy is illogically also under attack, as are sex education in schools and abortion clinics. The target list includes, in addition, homosexuality, sexual child abuse, incest, rape, date rape, and sexual harassment in the work place, all of which, no matter how reprehensive, are subject to exaggerated or false accusations that transcend genuine protection. Sexological surveys, even those designed to obtain data prerequisite to the containment of the HIV/AIDS epidemic, have been under political attack and have been legislatively and administratively suppressed and defunded.

Some counterreformationist targets overlap with the targets of at least some, though not all, feminists. The mainstream feminist movement has steered clear of antisexualism by adhering to the principle of the conceptual separation of gender from lust. Whenever lust has impinged too explicitly, it has been set aside for the attention of special interest organizations. In this way it has become possible to be a feminist either for or against pornography, for or against abortion, for or against safe sex, and so on. Nonfeminists have had the same option, and increasingly into the nineties young adult women have exercised that option without being self-identified as either for or against feminism.

To some extent, waning enthusiasm for mainstream feminism on the part of younger women in the early 1990s may be a concomitant of failure to address the apparent contradiction between equality of men and women on the dual criteria of gender and lust. Rather than sameness between men and women on the criterion of lust, there is reciprocity. The male-disparaging crusade of radical feminists helped by counterreformationists has become too strident, perhaps, for the generation of the nineties. Insofar as the infidels in this crusade are men, women may be held accountable for its stridency. Ironically, however, some of the crusaders are men. The secretive and self-righteous purpose of these male crusaders is to restore the prefeminist status quo by sacrificing some of their own sex in order to demonstrate that women are imperiled by men other than themselves. Simultaneously, this demonstrates that women are unable to be independent and autonomous, and must therefore be brought under the dependent protection of the likes of themselves. Scarlett O'Hara must live again!

Feminists who were once blinded by this ruse and who now see through it dissociate themselves from man-bashing tactics. The ultimate absurdity toward which man-bashing tactics lead is that of the disposable male, namely that, since only a few stud males will suffice for breeding, society could dispose of the rest. The stud males could thus be sequestered on a special lekking (from Swedish, *lek*, to play) estate, that is a kind of stud farm or male harem where men would wait for females to visit them, but only to be inseminated. In avian and mammalian lekking species, males assemble, on exhibit, to wait patiently to be selected. Lekking human males would be required to do the same. Other males would be disposed of as superfluous, in much the same way as male calves destined to become slaughtered or castrated for the meat market are segregated by dairy farmers and cattle ranchers from those destined to become stud bulls. For human beings, the impracticality of such a scenario is that the majority of men and women are not designed for such a way of life. Men and women do, indeed, become attracted to one another. They fall in love and become pairbonded. As members of mixed age groups, they also become troopbonded. Those are facts of phylogeny. They are inevitable exigencies of human existence.

Radical feminism's crusade against male sexuality, with female sexuality exempted, is unquestionably sexist. It perpetuates the social stereotype of the male as a sexually violent predator intent on using sex as an instrument of domination over unempowered women and juveniles. The extreme formulation of this male stereotype is the one that regards every act of sexual intercourse as an act of rape.

The sleight of hand by which male sexuality is equated with rape is counterproductive insofar as it provokes reactionary conservatism from the men's movement, instead of a conjoint struggle for equal rights. In radical feminist ideology it is not recognized as counterproductive, however, for it is consistent with the erroneous dogma that sex and gender are separate and nonoverlapping entities. Thus, in radical feminist ideology, it appears feasible to attack sexuality which is allegedly biologically determined and therefore immutable, without implicating gender which is allegedly socially constructed and mutable. According to this view, neutered gender, not sex, is the basis of male/female equality. The disparate male and female organs of procreation and their function are disregarded either as irrelevant, or as if they should be unisex, which is how radical feminism demands that gender should be.

Contemporary radical feminist theory incorporates Foucault's social constructionist theory not, as he had done, to expose the ideological relativity of the meaning of sexuality in history, but to expose the ideological relativity of the meaning of gender in contemporary lives. To deprive gender stereotypes of their erstwhile absoluteness by exposing their historical or cultural relativity is praiseworthy, but not at the cost of attempting to totally deconstruct the role of species phylogeny in influencing the developmental formation of those very stereotypes.

Deconstructionism carries the seeds of its own destruction, for the architect of deconstruction becomes the prophet of reconstruction only until he himself or she herself, in turn, is deconstructed. The outcome is eventual academic chaos, which has led some scholars to designate social constructionism as the new, postmodern, intellectual obscurantism. Gender and sex are two sides of the same coin which, if severed into two slices, is not a whole coin anymore.

Abuse and Deprivation in Childhood

The counterreformationist drift toward man-bashing shares its history with the history of parental abuse and neglect of children. There is no doubt a long history of parental kindness toward children, but there is an equally long history of parental cruelty, exploitation, deprivation, abusive discipline, and corporal punishment, all of which have been, until recently, within the legal rights of parenthood.

In the United States, the founding of the Society for the Prevention of Cruelty to Animals by Henry Berg in 1866 preceded by nearly a decade his founding of the Society for the Prevention of Cruelty to Children in 1875. The latter was precipitated by a case of pathological maternal cruelty and deprivation, that of nine-year-old Mary Ellen Wilson, which came to the attention of the authorities in New York City in 1874, and was much publicized in the *New York Times* (Williams and Money, 1980, chap. 8).

After the novelty of Mary Ellen's case wore off, society took no further action with respect to the abuse and deprivation of children by their parents for a full century until the passage of the Child Abuse Prevention and Treatment Act of 1974. In the interim, physicians and caseworkers had been seeing childhood injuries and suspecting or proving that they had been violently inflicted by parents on their own children. In some instances they were misled by the parents' alibis. Mostly, however, it was the prevailing philosophy of the sanctity of motherhood and the inviolacy of the family that blinded their professional judgment and misled them into formulating flimsy and erroneous explanations that would extricate health care professionals from having to act as medical police.

Professional complacency regarding child abuse did not survive the politically dissident era of the 1960s and its widespread and unrelenting questioning of the status quo. In 1962, Henry Kempe, Chairman of the Department of Pediatrics at the University of Colorado, published his rediscovery of parental child abuse under the title of the battered child syndrome (Kempe et al., 1980). Kempe's findings attracted widespread professional and media attention and led to nationwide state and federal legislation requiring mandatory reporting and intervention in cases of child abuse and neglect.

Initially the focus of child protection agencies was on physical battering which was evident in residual scars, cuts, tears, bruises, burns, bone fractures, and poisons. Their existence alone, however, does not prove that such signs have their origin in parental violence and abuse. Proof of parental culpability requires independent corroboration, which is all too often extremely difficult to obtain. It is equally, if not more difficult to obtain confirmatory evidence of parentally induced failure to thrive on the basis of systematic deprivation of nourishment, fluid, fresh air, toileting, sleep, bedding, clothing, and social contact. Parental abusiveness is a psychopathological syndrome in its own right with its own name, Munchausen syndrome by proxy, named by Money and Werlwas (1976) after a fictional narrator of fantastically unbelievable tales (Money, 1992). A person with Munchausen syndrome is a medical impostor who, having surreptitiously induced injury or disease either in the self, or by proxy in someone else, a child for example, fabricates a false medical history.

Like all impostors, medical impostors are, by definition, able to produce plausible alibis. In court, an expert defense attorney is thus able to pillory an expert witness who does not have absolute or irrefutable proof that a child's injury or illness was criminally induced by either parent, or both in collusion, and was not the result of an accident. This tactic, together with a wide reluctance to intrude on the rights of parenthood, allows the defense to win the case. The child is then returned home for more abuse.

Disheartened by such outrage and by its exorbitant demands on their time, pediatric health care providers and welfare caseworkers have progressively drifted away from the vigorous pursuit and reporting of suspected abusive cruelty and deprivation in childhood. But the same does not apply to suspected sexual abuse. Public sentiment against sexual abuse is so easily aroused that lack of confirmatory evidence is no hindrance to the inception of prosecution, even on the basis of false accusation.

Contingent on accusations of sexual abuse or molestation in childhood, a new profession and industry, victimology, has come into being within the criminal justice system. In support of the new industry of victimology, and in deference to pressure from the FBI, Public Law 98–292, the Child Protection Act of 1984 extended the legal age of childhood from sixteen to eighteen. This law expands the legal definition of child sexual abuse to include the private possession or showing of genital nudity of anyone below age eighteen in any medium. It includes, in addition to works of art, family snapshots of the new baby in the bathtub, for the possession of which even the parents or grandparents are liable to arrest. They may be reported by employees of photo-processing firms.

Victimology

The provisions of victimology are not so much for victims of disasters, calamities, or catastrophes of either human or natural origin, as for victims, euphemized as survivors, of child abuse or molestation, incest, rape including date rape, and wife abuse.

Rather than being a branch of medicine and science, victimology is a branch of law enforcement. A great many of its personnel have been recruited from the professional ranks of counseling and therapy in psychology and social case work. Although their primary allegiance is, by training, to the individual client or patient, by employment it is to the law enforcement agency that hires them or has a contract with them. Thus, they are de facto undercover police who obtain, on or from so-called perpetrators, confidential information that is subject to subpoena. Under mandatory reporting laws applicable especially to offenses against children, confidentiality does not exist, as information must be reported to officers of law enforcement. The offenses may be contemporary or retrospectively distant by as much as forty or fifty years. Fully grown adults may lay accusations against their own parents which, in many instances, are based on fabrications and the indoctrinations of misguided therapists and counselors acting as validators who practice disclosure therapy.

Victimology has not held itself scientifically accountable for various *obiter dicta* which it egregiously holds to be eternal verities such as, for example, that children never lie about sex; that ostensible memories recovered under duress are never false; that if you think you were sexually abused as a child, you were; and that memories of incest in infancy and childhood can be so completely repressed that they can be recovered in adulthood only under the influence of hypnosis or indoctrination therapy by validators.

Victimology's mistakes are not subject to the ordinary rules of scientific integrity or professional malpractice, but are played out according to the adversarial drama of the courtroom. Hence the possibility, ruthlessly realized, of brainwashing children to make confessions of sexual abuse and other fantastical brutalities of satanic rituals that never occurred, and never could have, in order to obtain a conviction of those falsely accused. The McMartin Preschool case in Manhattan Beach, California (Uncited, 1990; Eberle and Eberle, 1986), was the first large scale example of this phenomenon of manipulating children to make false confessions. This case is a twentieth-century equivalent of the Salem witch trials of 1690.

The proprietors and teachers of the school all were implicated by the complaint of a woman with a dual diagnosis of alcoholism and acute paranoid schizophrenia, who died in 1986 of an alcohol-related illness. In July of 1983, she told a physician that her two-and-a-half-year-old son had an itchy anus. She herself had at that time a vaginal infection and she wondered if she may have infected him. A few weeks later, she phoned the local police to report having noticed blood on his anus, and having heard him say something about a man named Ray. This man, whom the boy could not identify from a school photo, was a teacher at the nursery school he had briefly attended. The police required a medical examination. The intern at the hospital found the redness of the anal area "consistent with sodomy," but admitted having had no training in sexual abuse. The mother progressively embellished her accusations. She told the police that the teacher, Ray Buckey, had held her son's head in a toilet while he sodomized him. Wearing a mask and cape, he taped the boy's eyes, mouth and hands, and stuck an air tube up his rectum. He had made the boy ride naked on a horse, and he himself had dressed up as a child-molesting cop, a fireman, a clown, and a Santa Claus. She said that teachers at the school had jabbed scissors into the boy's eyes, and put staples in his ears, nipples, and tongue; Ray had pricked the boy's finger and put it in a goat's anus, and Ray's mother, Peggy Buckey, had killed a baby and made the boy drink the blood. As additional embellishments, the mother accused others of having sodomized her son; specifically, an AWOL marine, three health-club employees, the boy's own father from whom she was estranged, and the family dog. She also charged that three women at the McMartin Preschool were witches who had buried her son in a coffin; and one of them had killed a real baby, chopped open the head, and burned the brains.

The boy had attended the school for a total of only 14 days, and had been supervised by Ray Buckey only twice. The police searched Ray Buckey's apartment and the school, and found no incriminating evidence. Nonetheless, the 200 parents of the preschoolers were sent a police letter advising them to suspect oral sex, fondling of genitals, sodomy, and bondage if their child had been alone with Ray Buckey. Not one child disclosed anything suspicious.

Worried parents were referred by the prosecutors' office to the Children's International Institute (C.I.I.), an institution specialized in validating suspected sexual child abuse. The C.I.I. medical consultant advised parents that children at McMartin were probably abused. The children were interviewed by an unlicensed C.I.I. social worker, a self-appointed expert in child sexual abuse. Using puppets and "anatomically correct" dolls as stage properties and mouthpieces, this woman applied the standard brainwashing interview techniques for obtaining and videotaping enforced compliance and agreement with suggestions and conjectures. She offered the videotapes as professional proof that the children had been sexually abused.

Armed with the tapes, a politically ambitious assistant state's attorney convened a grand jury which gave him 208 charges involving 42 children. In the course of seven years, the prosecution spent up to an estimated $20 million on the case, and lost it. The jurors acquitted all of the preschool staff who had been indicted. Not only had the accusations been false, but they had been manufactured by professionals in the sex-abuse industry. These professionals are not held accountable for the tyrannous effect of their malpractice on not only those accused, but also the children. For seven years, beginning between the ages of three and five, these children had been held hostage to a fabricated biography in order to qualify for a possible very large sum of money in damages payments. To be brainwashed into incorporating a fabrication into one's biography is itself a form of traumatic abuse, and a source of psychopathology. The morbidity of its consequences persists for a lifetime.

Like other manifestations of group hysteria, the McMartin debacle was replicated across the nation and abroad, especially in English-speaking and predominantly Protestant nations. Together these replications demonstrate the power of victimology as a weapon of the forces of the antisexualism of the counterreformation.

In the theory and practice of victimology, perpetrators are predominantly men. Women perpetrators are considered the equivalent of witches. Victimology reinforces as well as reflects the split between sex as lust, and sex as gender. In victimology, especially in the popular media, lust is equated with masculine violence and metaphorically with "testosterone poisoning." It is ostensibly an attribute of all males. Females and juveniles are its victims.

In victimology, childhood sexual abuse is an etiological catchall for many different symptoms. It is, by definition, invariably experienced as traumatic stress, and its outcome, although variable, is diagnosed as post-traumatic stress disorder (PTSD). The symptoms of PTSD, it is claimed, may not appear concurrently with the stress, but be delayed in onset. When delayed, the experience of abuse is said to be repressed or "in denial." When it is recalled, however, the recall may prove to be, in fact, confabulation. Multiple personality disorder (MPD) is a too frequent diagnosis. The validity of MPD is much disputed by its opponents who attribute it to an iatrogenic (treatment-induced) origin. It is common that one of the MPD "alters" has a gender role, masculine or feminine, discordant with that of the other or others.

Freud's Early Seduction Theory Recycled

In its early years, before becoming entangled in forced confessions, fabricated memories, and false accusations of sexual abuse in satanic rituals, victimology had the appeal of directing attention legitimately, as it still may do, to epidemic neglect of the victimization of the defenseless—predominantly women and children.

Since the 1950s, in American child psychiatry women had been the victims of child psychiatric theory that scapegoated maternal deprivation and neglect and, for good measure, maternal overprotectiveness also, as the cause of all manner of child psychopathology. This scapegoating theory was psychoanalytically derived. When in the 1970s psychoanalysis came under feminist criticism, it was orthodox, not derivative psychoanalysis that was the target. Orthodox Freudian psychoanalysis was accused of perpetuating flagrant nineteenth-century Victorian sexism by continuing to depict the female as being psychologically a kind of male manqué, and destined by penis envy to be endemically masochistic and inferior to the male. This was a criticism which orthodox psychoanalysis could not refute, and also could not constrain. It proved to be the opening skirmish of what became an all-out war on psychoanalysis over the issue of the actuality versus the fantasy of sexual victimization in childhood, predominantly in females.

An early salvo was the publication by Schatzman (1973) of *Soul Murder: Persecution in the Family*, a reassessment of the Schreber case made famous by Freud. Niederland (1974) continued the assessment in *The Schreber Case: Psychoanalytic Profile of a Paranoid Personality*. Both of these publications gave credence to the actuality of the harsh postural training and disciplinary child-rearing practices imposed on Schreber by his somewhat fanatical physician father as being more plausibly significant for the son's later paranoid symptomatology than was Freud's inferential linkage of Schreber's paranoia to unconscious homosexual fantasies. Freudian theory was delivered a more crushing blow when Jeffrey Masson, at one time curator of the Freud Archives, published his attack, *The Assault on Truth: Freud's Suppression of the Seduction Theory* (1985), in which he accused Freud of fraudulence and expediency.

Seduction theory, as it came to be known had its origins in Freud's collaboration with Breuer on the treatment of psychoneurosis published as *Studies in Hysteria* (1885). The next year, Freud (1896) published a journal article, "The Etiology of Hysteria," in which he enlarged upon his newly formulated theory of the retrospective origin of hysterical symptoms in infantile sexual scenes and sexual intercourse in childhood. Freud was quite explicit in specifying that he was referring to rape, abuse, seduction, attack, assault, aggression, and trauma. He wrote:

> All the singular conditions under which the ill-matched pair conduct their love-relations—on the one hand the adult, who cannot escape his share in the mutual dependence necessarily entailed by a sexual relationship, and who is yet armed with complete authority and the right to punish, and can exchange the one role for the other to the uninhibited satisfaction of his moods, and on the other hand the child, who in his helplessness is at the mercy of this arbitrary will, who is prematurely aroused to every kind of sensibility and exposed to every sort of disappointment, and whose performance of the sexual activities assigned to him is often interrupted by his imperfect control of his natural needs—all these grotesque and yet tragic incongruities reveal themselves as stamped upon the later development of the individual and of his neurosis, in countless permanent effects which deserve to be traced in the greatest detail (Masson, 1985, pp. 283–84).

Freud's satisfaction with his seduction theory was short-lived. It was scarcely a year old when, in the fall of 1897, he abandoned it. Possibly he had been insidiously influenced by the skepticism of fellow professionals of whom he wrote to his friend Wilhelm Fliess as follows.

> A lecture on the etiology of hysteria at the Psychiatric Society [April 26, 1896] met with an icy reception from the asses and from Krafft-Ebing the strange comment: It sounds like a scientific fairy tale. And this after one has demonstrated to them a solution to a more than thousand year old problem, a source of the Nile! They can all go to hell (Masson, 1985, p. 9).

Irrespective of insidious influence, it was nonetheless inherent in the very nature of seduction theory itself that Freud, megalomanic theory builder that he was, would become dissatisfied. The theory was conceptually too constricting. It failed to account for the development of psychoneurosis in the absence of a history of sexual seduction in childhood. It relied too heavily on fortuity in the ontogeny of individual development, at the expense of regularity in the phylogeny of species development. Its causality was extrinsic to the organism, not intrinsic to it.

Freud might have resolved his dissatisfaction with seduction theory by keeping it paired with hysterical neurosis in a taxonomical system in which, as in the case of the *aktuell* neuroses (neurasthenia and anxiety), which Freud classified as contemporary not retrospective in origin, each type of neurosis would have its own etiology. This would have rescued the long-term manifestations of traumatic sexual seduction in childhood from the professional neglect that became their fate for more than half a century.

The route by which Freud resolved his dissatisfaction with seduction theory was not by taxonomy, but by new theorizing. He postulated that, in the psychoneuroses (hysterical and obsessional), the revelations of seduction pertained not to the early history of behavioral acts, but to the early history of mental imagery and ideation in fantasies and dreams, and in the unconscious. By universalizing this postulate, infantile seduction fantasies became the basis of an all-encompassing, comprehensive theory that would be both phylogenetic and endopsychic in origin. In other words, it would be applicable to all members of the human race, and its principles would be consistently of the mind or, in German, of the soul (*Seele*). It would explain mental health as well as pathology. It would become not just the theory of the Oedipus complex, but in its widest scope the entire psychoanalytic theory of all of human nature. Although its constructs would resemble those of the Biblical theory of human nature, it would be, above all, a secular alternative to theological theories of human nature.

Being secular, psychoanalytic theory was destined to have immense appeal among the erudite of a scientifically secular twentieth century. It would also invite attack. Its Achilles' heel would prove to be the very seduction theory that it had set aside. Insofar as there was no setting aside of the actualities and the sequelae of seduction and sexual trauma experienced in the lives of some children, seduction theory would eventually be recycled.

In the recycled version of seduction theory, trauma replaces seduction as the defining concept, and posttraumatic stress disorder (a term popularized during the Vietnam War) replaces hysterical neurosis as the diagnostic outcome. In the interval between the period of traumatization and the onset of treatment, if the victim of alleged sexual abuse has no recollection of its having occurred, then repression is invoked to explain the absence of recall. Thus, recall or its opposite, failure of recall, are both accepted as proof that sexual abuse did occur. In the case of failure of recall, the professional validator is charged with the duty of coaxing recall under duress, and implanting suggestions until false recall is fabricated. The fabrication has been named the false memory syndrome. This syndrome may be induced in children of kindergarten age, so that they fabricate abuse that did not actually occur. The syndrome may also be induced in adults in mid-life so that they fabricate memories of child abuse (usually incest) that did not actually occur in their own childhood.

Victimology uses recycled seduction theory as a substitute for psychoanalytic or any other theory of psychopathology and psychotherapy, and applies it to explain a very wide range of symptoms of lack of well-being, including bodily symptoms and depression.

The revival of Freud's seduction theory and the reclassification of seduction as sexual child abuse is overtly related to the radical feminist attack on the sexuality of not just a pathological minority of men, but of all men, as an expression of coercive power over women. In *The Assault on Truth*, Jeffrey Masson quite explicitly aligns himself with radical feminists and their victimology position, namely, that they are the victims and men are the perpetrators of sexual molestation and abusive coercion. By implicit, but unprovable assumption, if men relinquish sexual domination over women, women will not exercise sexual domination over men. In other words, lust will be neutralized, and without lust, gender—male and female—will be egalitarian. The alternative possibility, not well considered in feminist theory, is an escalation of adversarialism and conflict in the relationship between men and women. If men assert dominance over women, as they do in religiously fundamentalist politics, and if women become deemancipated, then the crusade of the counterreformation will have succeeded in reversing the clock and returning manhood and womanhood to the earlier status quo of inequality. The more likely outcome of the crusade, however, is an escalation of the conflict betwen manhood and womanhood, into the twenty-first century.

· 6 ·

Gendermaps

Imprinting
Terminology
Multivariate Sequential Determinants
Hypothalamic Sexual Dimorphism
Homosexual/Heterosexual Dimorphism
Gender Bias
Juvenile Development
Adolescence

· 6 ·

Gendermaps

Imprinting

At every stage of development, nothing is purely nature, and nothing is purely nurture (see chap. 2). There is always a collaboration between the two. At the outset, nature is encoded within the genome which, from the beginning, is dependent on the nurturing environment provided by the ovum and sperm. After the ovum and sperm unite, nurturing of the genome is provided by the community of proliferating cells, and by the protection of the womb. Sometimes the timing of the nature/nurture collaboration is stringently limited to a critical developmental period. Before the onset of that critical period it is too soon for a particular stage of development to take place, and after the ending of the critical period too late. Moreover, whatever the consequence of development that fails or is erroneous during the critical period, it is fixed and irreversible. There is no backtracking and starting again for a second time.

Critical periods of development are both prenatal and postnatal. Postnatally they may apply to the type of development that, in the vernacular, is loosely called learning. The development of native language is one example, and the development of masculinity/femininity is another. Critical period learning is usually called imprinting. It requires a brain that has developed ahead of time so as to possess a highly specific recognition schema which, when stimulated by a matching input stimulus, releases a highly specific output response. Imprint learning becomes fixed in the brain and is resistant to "unlearning" so that it may be retained for a lifetime. Once an imprint is fixed in the brain, it functions as nature, not nurture. Regardless of how it originated, it becomes a component of the biology of the brain. That is why it is possible to say that the eyes, ears, and other senses are able to program the brain just as immutably as are genes or hormones. Whereas it is important to know what gets built into the brain, as well as how it gets there, it is even more important to know how immutably it becomes fixed in the brain once it gets in.

The idea that something can enter the brain from outside (i.e., from nurture) and then become incorporated into the brain (i.e., equated with nature) is of profound importance in understanding the multivariate and sequential development and differentiation of masculinity/femininity in the gendermap.

Terminology

Gendermap is the term used to refer to the entity, template, or schema within the mind and brain (mindbrain) unity, that codes masculinity and femininity and androgyny. The gendermap overlaps with the lovemap and codes the lovemap as masculine, feminine, or bisexual. The lovemap includes a wide range of sexuoerotic ideation, imagery, and practice that is not necessarily gender coded. By contrast, the gendermap includes a wide range of nonsexuoerotic ideation, imagery, and practice that is, like education, vocation, and recreation, coded as masculine, feminine, or androgynous. The formal definitions of gendermap and lovemap are as follows:

> **gendermap:** a developmental representation or template synchronously in the mind and brain depicting the details of one's gender-identity/role (G-I/R). It includes the lovemap but is larger, insofar as it incorporates whatever is gender coded vocationally, educationally, recreationally, sartorially, and legally, as well as in matters of etiquette, grooming, body language, and vocal intonation.

> **lovemap:** a developmental representation or template synchronously in the mind and in the brain depicting the idealized lover, the idealized love affair, and the idealized program of sexuoerotic activity projected in imagery or actually engaged in with the lover.

The gendermap and the lovemap are, in human beings, rather like the native languagemap. The healthy brain is prepared for them before birth, but their full development requires social input after birth. The gendermap and the lovemap both are conceptual entities that comprise ideation, imagery, and behavioral practices. They are part of an entire library of mindbrain maps, among which are, for example, foodmaps, agemaps, healthmaps, childcaremaps, and so on.

The gendermap is a conceptual entity under which are assembled all the male/female differences, and similarities also, not only those that are procreative and phylogenetically determined, but also those that are arbitrary and conventionally determined, such as male/female differences in education, vocation, and recreation. The gendermap and lovemap each have a history of growth and development from very simple beginnings to very complex outcomes. They are multivariately and sequentially determined and, therefore, complicated to study. Explanations of their genesis are in terms of temporal sequences, not causal sequences.

Multivariate Sequential Determinants

Figure 1 shows the variables of male/female differentiation in sequence. Some variables are phylogenetically transmitted and some are socially transmitted. Neither biological nor social construction is exclusive. The gendermap is an integrated product of both.

When an earlier version of Figure 1 was first constructed for lecture use in 1970, the topmost entry was chromosomal sex, XX (female) and XY (male), and the second entry was gonadal sex. The presence of the Y chromosome ensured that, by the sixth week of embryonic life, an undifferentiated cluster of cells would be instructed to differentiate as a testis, not an ovary. In 1977 it was discovered that the Y chromosome ensured also that a serologically detectable cell surface protein, named H-Y antigen, would organize the development of the embryonic testes (Silvers and Wachtel, 1977; Ohno, 1978).

In pursuit of the gene responsible for formation of the embryonic testes, Page et al. (1987) located a testis determining factor (TDF) or region on the Y chromosome. The actual gene, named SRY for the sex determining region of the Y chromosome, was identified three years later by Sinclair et al. (1990).

The developmental priority of the embryo is to become differentiated morphologically as a female which is what happens, irrespective of chromosomal sex, unless a masculinizing principle is added. That principle is supplied in the form of sex hormones, supplied by the fetal testes, beginning at around the third month of pregnancy. No corresponding supply of sex hormones from the fetal ovaries is needed for feminization. The possible role of placental and maternal female hormones has not been ascertained.

Convergent Multivariate Sequential Determinism of the Gendermap

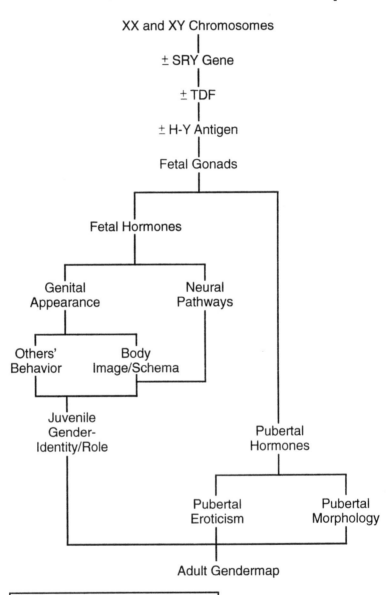

LEGEND:
SRY=Sex-Determining Region Y Chromosome
TDF=Testis Determining Factor

One of the two hormones secreted by the fetal testis is MIH (mullerian inhibiting hormone). Its fetal influence is brief, and its function is a defeminizing one, namely suppression of the minuscule mullerian ducts that would otherwise act as precursors from which form the uterus and fallopian tubes. The other hormone from the fetal testis is masculinizing. It has three names: male or masculinizing hormone, androgen (from Greek, *andros*, man), and testosterone (from Latin, *testis*). In prenatal life its function is first to program the growth of the internal male structures (the epididymis, *vas deferens*, prostate, and seminal vesicles) bilaterally from their precursors, the minuscule wolffian ducts; and then to program the undifferentiated precursors of the external sexual organs to differentiate as male instead of female. To form the external sexual organs, testosterone interacts with the enzyme, 5α-reductase within the cells of the undifferentiated precursor structures to form dihydrotestosterone, the hormone that they need in order to differentiate into the external genital anatomy of the male. In this process, the genital tubercle becomes a penis with a foreskin and a skin-covered urinary tube, and not a clitoris with a hood and two labia minora. The external swellings become fused to form the wrinkled scrotum, and not the two unfused, smooth labia majora.

As already mentioned in chapter 2, the principle of adding something to obtain masculinization applies also to sexually dimorphic nuclei and pathways of the brain (Tobet and Fox, 1992). Testosterone again is the responsible hormone. Surprisingly enough, however, it must first be changed within brain cells by being aromatized by the enzyme, aromatase, into estradiol. The surprise is that estradiol performs a masculinizing function, for elsewhere in the body it brings about feminization and is pharmacologically classified as a female hormone.

Brain masculinization takes place after, not before the masculinization of the external genitalia. In some species of laboratory animals, the timing of brain masculinization is shortly before birth, and in others in the immediate postnatal period. In the human species the exact timing has not been experimentally determined, due to ethical constraints on human experimentation. Although it may begin prenatally, it is more likely that the timing of human brain masculinization is, by inference, in the early postnatal period. As adumbrated in chapter 2, the rationale for this inference is that, between the second and twelfth weeks after birth, there is in male but not in female infants a surge of testosterone that, measured in a blood sample, reaches a high level that it will not reach again until puberty (Migeon and Forest, 1983).

No corresponding hormonal surge has been observed in females. It is known from laboratory studies of neonatal rats, however, that the level of the neurotransmitter, serotonin, in the brain's hypothalamic region (see below) is higher in females than males in the newborn period; and that this difference correlates with behavioral feminization and demasculinization of mating and other responses in adulthood (Wilson et al., 1986, 1991; Farabollini et al., 1988).

Hypothalamic Sexual Dimorphism

In animal brain research, it is easier to discover male/female differences in neuroanatomical structures than it is to discover what function they serve. Structures in the region of the hypothalamus are those that have been implicated in governing procreative behavior and its difference in males and females. The hypothalamus is situated deep in the brain behind the bridge of the nose. It is connected with the pituitary gland, which is suspended and cradled in the *sella turcica* below it. Only pea-sized, the hypothalamus participates in a remarkably wide range of vital functions and has a veritable information highway of connections in the adjacent limbic system or paleocortex and in the neocortex, above.

The posterior region of the hypothalamus has an intimate neurohormonal relationship with the pituitary gland in regulating the secretion of pituitary hormones (gonadotropins) that, from puberty onward, circulate in the bloodstream and upon reaching the gonads (ovaries and testicles) in turn regulate their hormonal secretions, namely, estrogen and progesterone from the ovaries, and testosterone from the testicles.

Bilaterally, in the anterior region of the hypothalamus is located the sexually dimorphic nucleus (SDN) of the preoptic area (POA). In males the SDN/POA is larger than in females, for which reason it was named sexually dimorphic. The origin of its larger size in the male has been traced in animal studies to the influence of masculinizing hormone (in this case testosterone, aromatized to estradiol) normally produced from the fetal testes during a critical period that, according to species, is either just before or just after birth. The same hormone may be necessary to prevent cell shrinkage in the SDN/POA postpubertally. In rat studies the neurotransmitter, serotonin, has also been implicated (Handa et al., 1986). In laboratory animals, SDN/POA function has been shown to be intimately connected with complex male/female differences in courtship and mating behavior, chiefly crouching or presenting (lordosis) by females, and mounting by males.

Houtsmuller and colleagues (1993) in A.K. Slob's laboratory at Erasmus University, Rotterdam, found that the volume of the SDN/POA in male rats was permanently diminished by perinatal treatment with the aromatase-inhibitor, ATD, a substance that blocks the conversion of testosterone to estradiol, which hormone is necessary for masculinization of the SDN/POA. Perinatal treatment with ATD also demasculinized the rats' subsequent sexual behavior and reduced their responsiveness to an estrous female in favor of a normal male. The degree of demasculinization of the size of the SDN/POA was correlated with the degree of demasculinization and feminization of reproductive behavior.

The male and female patterns of courtship and mating behavior in subprimate mammals are species specific and are replicated by all members of the species. One may think of individuals of these species as hormonal robots whose courtship and mating patterns are hormonally programmed perinatally for life, with some but not much likelihood of being altered by the intrusion of postnatal influences in the prepubertal years particularly.

In subhuman primates, there is less prenatal hormonal robotism, and more postnatal flexibility for the incorporation of influences individually absorbed from variations in the social environment, such as being reared in isolation instead of in a troop.

Among primates, human beings show the least evidence of prenatal hormonal robotization, and the most evidence of the overlay of postnatal programming on the behavior of courtship and mating. Thus, it may not be taken for granted that male/female differences in nuclei of the human anterior hypothalamus (see reviews by Hooper, 1992; Swaab et al., 1992) are attributable exclusively to prenatal hormonal programming, with no incorporation of superimposed postnatal programming of hormonal or any other origin.

Homosexual/Heterosexual Dimorphism

Postnatal programming has particular significance with respect to a neuroanatomical difference in some hypothalamic structures of male brains to which has been attributed the difference between being homosexual and heterosexual. One such structure is the suprachiasmic nucleus (SCN) (Swaab et al., 1992), and another the third interstitial nucleus of the anterior hypothalamus (INAH-3) (LeVay, 1991, 1993). In addition, a third homosexual/heterosexual difference has been found in the size of the anterior commissure (AC), a fiber tract joining the right and left sides of the brain in the vicinity of the anterior hypothalamus (Allen and Gorski, 1992). The right and left sides of the brain are joined also by the *corpus callosum*. Although no homosexual/heterosexual difference in the size of this organ has been reported, the absence of a difference between female-to-male transexuals and normal controls has been reported by Bosinski et al. (1994).

The three positive findings above were that in homosexual brains the SCN was larger, the INAH-3 smaller, and the AC larger than in heterosexual brains. In all three studies the autopsied brains were from male organ donors, some of whom, heterosexual and homosexual, had died of AIDS, and some of other causes. All three studies await replication before they can be accepted with confidence. If they are replicated, the research challenge will remain of tracing their origins to their sources in prenatal or postnatal molecular biology, or both. If they originate prenatally, then one possibility is that their source can be traced to the DNA of the genome—specifically to an X-linked locus, Xq28, on the long arm of the X chromosome (inherited from the mother) according to research on the genetics of homosexuality in males (Hamer et al., 1993). Hamer and his coworkers found a linkage between homosexuality and polymorphic markers on Xq28 in 64 percent of forty pairs of gay brothers. They also found, in another sample of 114 homosexual men and their kinships, an increased rate of homosexuality in males in the maternal line, namely, among maternal uncles and among cousins who were sons of maternal aunts.

The likelihood that a single gene or gene complex codes for so multiplex and variable an entity as sexual orientation in the absence of a cascade of intervening variables is untenable. The prenatal genetic and hormonal precursors of male/female differences in the behavior of human courtship and mating, either homosexual or heterosexual, are not the finished product. They are precursors only on which, developmentally, more will be overlaid.

Gender Bias

Postnatally the developmental social overlay is differentiated as either masculine or feminine right from the moment of birth when the sex is announced as either boy or girl. Without being explicitly aware of doing so, people comport themselves with gender bias toward the newborn. Nothing more is needed to evoke a bias toward responding to a baby as a boy or a girl than to have been told that it is either, respectively, a boy or a girl, even if the baby is the same one in each instance. This bias has been demonstrated experimentally, but it also occurs routinely in everyday life. To ensure that no mistakes are made girls are dressed in pink and boys in blue.

The stereotypes of gender bias are age graded so as to reciprocate a child's own developmental stage of gender-biased comportment. It is a two-way street, of course, for in reciprocity each influences the other. That is why it is easy to take your own gender-biased stereotypes so much for granted that you seem only to be responding to, not influencing the masculinity or femininity of the child. But influence them you do, day in, day out, and so does everyone else whom the child encounters. Masculinity and femininity cannot develop in a social vacuum any more than can native language. Languages vary by dialect and accent, as well as in individual usage. So also, gender comportment varies not only individually, but also geographically, regionally and locally, according to cultural stereotypes of what constitutes masculinity and femininity.

For all the people in a baby's life, the criterion of the baby's sex is the anatomy of the external genitalia. For the baby, the criterion of the developmental masculinity/femininity of the baby's own body image is likewise the anatomy of the external genitalia. The genital body image is constructed of tactual and visual components. Its representation in the brain is presumably in the same region of the cerebral cortex as the representation of the genital body schema. However, the map in the brain of the body image in its entirety is still pretty much a scientific *terra incognita*. Its significance is made evident in the syndrome of transexualism. In the transexual's body image, the representation of the natal genitalia is alien, and there is a fixation on having them surgically changed from male to female, or from female to male, to agree with the body image.

In the infantile and juvenile years, children encounter the four categories of gender difference presented in chapter 3. Variously combined and permutated, components from each of these four categories become progressively fitted or mapped together into a personal gendermap. The gendermap codes masculine and feminine not separately, but as a pair. In most people one of the pair is coded as mine, and the other as thine. Without the feminine schema, males would lack cues for interacting with females, and without the masculine schema, females would lack cues for interacting with males. The two schemas in some people, impersonators with dual personalities, for example, alternate episodically. In others they may change places and remain transposed for an indefinite period of time, examples of which are transexualism and gynemimesis (miming women, but without undergoing reconstructive transexual surgery).

As in the formations of a geological map, the formations of a gendermap begin with the primordial strata and contours onto which other features are superimposed. Each additional formation becomes incorporated into the structure of the gendermap as a whole which then, in turn, becomes the foundation for the next addition. Formations that are socially constructed become welded into the total structure where they may become as fixed and immutable as if they had been, to use common parlance, exclusively genetic or biological and nonsocial in origin. These formations become biologically inbuilt into the mindbrain by way of the biology of learning and remembering. For this reason, it is not possible to subdivide the gendermap into features that are either exclusively biological or exclusively social in origin. However, there are some features that are phylogenetically shared with other members of the species, and some that are ontogenetically personal.

Juvenile Development

In many nonhuman species including sheep (see chap. 2), but especially in primate species, juvenile sexual rehearsal play is a phylogenetic feature of the development of what in human beings is termed the gendermap. Rhesus monkeys reared in social isolation so that they are deprived of social play, including mounting and thrusting in the course of sexually cavorting around are unable, postpubertally, to position themselves and to be cooperative in sexual intercourse, even with a gentle and experienced partner. Play-deprived females in whom pregnancy is experimentally induced become abusive and neglecting as mothers. They may kill the baby. Juveniles who are allowed as little as a half hour of play daily do better at rehearsing for breeding in adulthood, but only after six to twelve months' delay, and in only a third of cases. Those animals that do breed have a diminished birth rate (reviewed in Money, 1986, chap. 39; 1988a, pp. 62–66).

The gender stereotypes that we live by in rearing our children do not legitimize juvenile sexual rehearsal play either solo, in pairs, or in groups. Transculturally, however, there is some evidence that tolerance instead of intolerance of juvenile sexual rehearsal play is conducive to, and certainly compatible with the formation of gendermaps free from pathological distortions.

One transcultural example is provided by the Aboriginal inhabitants of Arnhem Land on the Australian north central coast (Money et al.,

1970). Traditionally, they have no intolerance of age-concordant juvenile sexual rehearsal play, which is one of their ancient traditions that has initially survived westernized acculturation. Once in a while in nursery school at nap time a boy and a girl might lie side by side and front to back, his body making pelvic thrusting movements against her rear, as innocuously as if rocking or thumbsucking. Aboriginal children a year or two older, aged five or six, may play at more explicit coital positioning when going to sleep outdoors around the traditional campfire. Adults pay no heed, or may be amused, as if to say: "They will know what to do when they grow up."

It is not clear whether children invent such positioning play in the absence of a model to copy or whether they mimic the play of children a bit older. They may see adolescents and adults copulating, although even in Aboriginal Australia that is not likely. Adults typically copulate in private, usually in the dark. Among the adults, there is no evidence of a deleterious effect from sexual play in their own childhood. On the contrary, it may have had a beneficial effect on sexological health since there was no evidence of paraphilia (kinky sex) impinging on their gendermaps. There was also no evidence of transposition from heterosexual to bisexual or homosexual in their gendermaps, which is surprising in view of the transcultural ubiquity of such transposition.

If juvenile sexual rehearsal play has no deleterious effect in a society in which it is tolerated, then the reverse must be considered, namely that deprivation of such play in a society in which it is not tolerated, but prohibited and punished, does have a deleterious effect. A scientifically designed epidemiological survey that would settle this issue cannot be implemented so long as today's counterreformatory dogma prevails in society and in government and prevents it. In the histories of people in clinics for sexual dysfunction or in courtrooms for sexual offenses, however, one repetitively finds that sexual pathology of all types, from harmlessly private to criminally offensive, has its origin in the juvenile years. Although information about the juvenile origin of sexual pathology has been obtained prospectively (Money and Lamacz, 1989), retrospective ascertainment predominates.

A common etiological principle in adult sexual pathology is deprivation of normal sexual information and learning in childhood and suppression of normal age-appropriate sexual rehearsal play (alone or together) in preparation for normal maturity. Especially if compounded by severe penalties and humiliation for sexual transgressions, juvenile sexual deprivation and suppression qualify as an antisexual form of child abuse and neglect.

Another etiological principle in adult sexual pathology is contradiction and inconsistency in childhood between, on the one hand, sexual deprivation and prohibition, and on the other hand, sexual sophistication and participation. This combination entraps a child with no escape from a Catch-22 dilemma in which "you're damned if you do and damned if you don't" admit or disclose being in the trap. This type of Catch-22 applies also to sharing and participating in normal age-concordant sexual information and play. Such experiences are prerequisite to social acceptance by age-mates, and at the same time are subject to being penalized by adults.

A Catch-22 applies also to age-discordant sexually explicit relationships that may not be traumatizing, per se, but have severely traumatizing criminal justice consequences for both parties if discovered or revealed.

The Catch-22 dilemma is bedeviling in sexually explicit encounters that, even if age-concordant and consensual, are coercively one-sided, as in many sadomasochistic or bondage and discipline relationships, for example. However, intervention to rescue the coerced partner from one-sided compliance enforced by threat, torture, sadistic assault, violent injury, or possible murder is indisputably necessary. Rescue in some instances is rendered peculiarly difficult by reason of the paradoxical phenomenon of collusion with the abuser and addiction to abuse.

This collusional phenomenon is known as the Stockholm syndrome. It is named for one of four female hostages of Jan-Erik Olson, a thirty-two-year-old bank robber who held up the Sveriges Kreditbank in Stockholm in 1973. She became slavishly enamored of and pairbonded to the man who held her hostage with a machine gun. When freed, she broke with her fiancé and married Olson (Streutz, quoted in Musaph, 1994).

The hostage who married Olson may well have become involved in an affair with him while still held captive, which would be in keeping with the general principle that a sexuoerotic outcome typically has a sexuoerotic beginning. This principle applies developmentally: the sexuoerotic features of both the gendermap and lovemap as manifested in adolescence, anomalies included, have their antecedents earlier in prepuberty. The childhood antecedent need not be specifically genital sexual abuse, although it might appear that way if one pays attention only to contemporary media hype. Sexuoeroticism involves close tactual intimacy and personalized bonding, both of which have their antecedents in earliest infancy. Prolonged deprivation or pathological excess of intimacy and bonding in infancy and childhood may adversely affect gendermap and lovemap development. So also may periodic betrayal of

intimacy and bonding, or their sudden and catastrophic actual or threatened loss by separation or illness and death. In such as case, developmental distortion of the gendermap/lovemap may constitute a symbolic
restitution. Children and adolescents whose gendermaps and lovemaps
are pathologically distorted prove, time and time again, to have an antecedent history of having grown up in a household afflicted with inter-
personal and sexuoerotic pathology.

Adolescence

The major features of the gendermap are fixed by the end of the prepubertal years, although their dimensions will change under the influence
of the hormonally induced changes of puberty and adolescence. As the
body matures into adulthood, it changes the comportment of other
people towards the self. The body image also changes, usually concor-
dantly with the actual body. But there are exceptions when the body and
the body image are discordant as, for example, on the criterion of age,
gender, or cosmetic appeal.

The hormones of puberty do not dictate whether an individual's
gendermap will orient that individual toward other people heterosexu-
ally, homosexually, or bisexually. However, the hormones of puberty do
maximize both the amplitude and frequency of an individual's ideation
and imagery of erotic attraction, yearning, and lust, whether normophilic,
paraphilic, hypophilic, or hyperphilic.

The hormones of puberty also maximize the gendermap's amplitude
and frequency with respect to the ideation and imagery of parenthood
which, for the female gendermap includes pregnancy. At the same time,
society promises, not always in good faith, to underwrite the gendermap's
ideation and imagery of independence and vocational achievement. In
accordance with gender stereotypes of extreme antiquity, society's prom-
ise is strongly gender biased. For adolescent girls, the bias disfavors
gendermaps in which an extramural (nondomestic) career is dominant
over pregnancy, parenthood, and a domestic career. For adolescent boys,
the bias is the other way round. Society is biased against the gendermap
of house-husbandhood. In today's world, there are more young women
whose gendermaps carry powerful ideation and imagery of a
nondomestic career than there are young men whose gendermaps include
a domestic career.

This imbalance has, in the ultimate analysis, been responsible for the
conceptual separation of gender from sex in vernacular usage and in the

philosophy of mainstream feminism. It has also fueled radical feminism's attack on masculinity into a war in which male dominance over women is equated not simply with power and aggression, but with pornography, harassment, and rape.

· 7 ·

Mismatched Gendermaps

Identification/Complementation
Falling in Love: Limerence
Reciprocality: Career Compatibility
Reciprocality: Sexuoerotic Orientation
Paraphilic Lovemaps

· 7 ·

Mismatched Gendermaps

Identification/Complementation

A fter the earliest years of infancy, coding of the gendermap in the human mind and brain shrinks from more to less bipotentiality and toward masculine or feminine monopotentiality. After the early years, gendermap coding is no longer mediated exclusively by hormonal or other neurotransmitter substances in the brain (chap. 6). Instead gendermap coding is increasingly mediated by informational input from the social environment through the senses—haptic (tactual), olfactory, and to some extent gustatory, at first, and then predominantly auditory and visual. From late infancy onwards, boys assimilate boyhood and girls girlhood into their gendermaps predominantly in conformity with the societal ideology and the stereotypes of the family, the community, and the culture in which they live. They do so in accordance with two great principles, identification and complementation.

Identification means imitating, hero-worshiping, and assimilating phenomena from people of the same declared sex as one's own, whether parent, other kin, older sibling, age-mate, or whomever else, even a television star, who has been adopted as a role model. Complementation means projecting onto a parent, other kin, older sibling, age-mate, or anyone else who has been adopted as a suitable reciprocating partner, everything that has been attained through identification. Thus, the little girl flirts with her daddy, and her little brother plays escort to his mommy.

Identification and complementation continue throughout childhood and beyond. One manifestation of peergroup identification and complementation is in the sexually dimorphic roles of juvenile sexual rehearsal play, a developmental phenomenon common to the young of primate species (see chap. 6).

In the developmental coding of the gendermap of both boys and girls, masculine and feminine are dualistically represented as positive and negative. The positive pole codes for me, for who I am, boy or girl. The negative pole codes for not me, for who I am not, girl or boy, respectively. At each pole there is a map or schema of what is coded there, one labeled feminine, and the other masculine. Everybody, boy and girl, man and woman, has both maps, one depicting "me," and the other depicting "thee." If the two maps change places, then one has a gender transposition disorder. One map may displace the other, as in full-blown transexualism, or both may coexist in alternation as a phenomenon of dual personality, one masculine and one feminine. Another possibility is that the two maps may merge in some degree of androgyny or bisexuality.

Under ordinary circumstances of development, one expects concordance between the prenatal and the postnatal coding of an individual's gendermap. In addition, one expects that the gendermap will be concordant with the natal sex of the external genitalia. Under circumstances in which the gendermap is discordant with the natal sex of the external genitalia, the source of discordancy may lie in either the prenatal or the postnatal coding of the gendermap, or in both combined.

Falling in Love: Limerence

In everyday idiom, it is said that someone falls in love, even at first sight, with someone else—a live person, usually, not a photograph, painting, or sculpture. That person may be defined metaphorically as a loveblot. By analogy with an inkblot in a Rorschach test, a loveblot is a person who serves as a stimulus onto whom one projects the combined imagistic content of one's own gendermap and lovemap. This projection is enabled to take place because there is some degree of correspondence between the person-as-loveblot and the image of the lover and love affair embodied in one's own idealized gendermap and lovemap. Then ensues the omnipotence of the concept that love conquers all. This is a false concept except when, like the two sides of the same coin, the lovemaps of the two persons are reciprocally perfect matches, blemishes and all. Then each person is a reciprocally matching loveblot for the lovemap of the other.

When each lover reciprocates and fulfills the imagery of the other, then the erotosexual pairbonding of falling in love is likely to be long-lasting, regardless of whether the match is orthodox and typical or unorthodox and atypical. For example, when a male-to-female impersonator (or gynemimetic) falls in love with a man who has the syndrome of gynemimetophilia, that is of being able to fall in love and to pairbond only with a lady with a penis, then the relationship may indeed be prolonged, even until death claims one partner first. There are many different but analogous relationships—consensual sadism and masochism, for example.

Limerence is the term that signifies the state of being love stricken. It may also signify the state of being love sick. The term *limerence* was coined by Dorothy Tennov in 1979. Being limerent appears to be a peculiarly human experience for which there is no easily accessible animal model. Limerence has only two other counterparts in human experience, grief and religious ecstasy. All three may be abruptly sudden in onset, overwhelming in their intensity, fixatedly long-lasting, unresponsive to logical reasoning, and capable of leading to wildly irrational acts of self-sabotage.

The chemistry of love is a popular concept that surfaces annually in the media in advance of St. Valentine's Day each February. Attributing the experience of limerence to chemistry is an attempt to explain what is involuntary and otherwise mysterious. In the ultimate analysis, of course, limerence is mediated by neurochemistries of the brain, although what those chemistries are, and what their action is, remains to be ascertained. One speculation is that they belong in the class of catecholamines which, like amphetamine, produce a high. One in particular, phenylethylalanine, has been named (Liebowitz, 1983). It is found also in chocolate, a favorite Valentine gift!

Getting high from the brain chemistries of love may one day explain why some people are love junkies who ride the wave of one love affair to the next, reiteratively. Their highs are very high, and their lows very low.

Limerence is the subjective experience of what is empirically observable as lover-lover pairbonding. Pairbonding between lovers is one of the characteristics of our species that underwrites the next generation. It guarantees that two people will be at the high intensity of a love affair for on the average a couple of years if not longer. Two years is long enough for being in love to lead to pregnancy and delivery, with both parents together and available for infant care. The baby's survival is contingent on its becoming pairbonded with, at a minimum, the mother or, in her absence, a substitute who provides nourishment and care. Thus, the two-way bond between the parents must open up and become a three-way bond that includes the infant.

This process is repeated with each new delivery. As time passes, the leaping flames of the initial love affair are likely to become the bright embers of conjugal love which, while being different, need not necessarily be experienced as inferior. There are some people for whom long-term monogamous family life is destined to be fully rewarding, but that is not the destiny of all members of the human race.

Falling in love with a pairbondedness that lasts through adolescence into adulthood may take place as early as age eight (Money, 1980, pp. 148–49). For most people, however, the age of the first love affair is in adolescence, after the onset of puberty. In the young, if a love affair meets with family and community disapproval, it is trivialized by being stigmatized as puppy love or infatuation. The term *infatuation* is also used when a second or multiple love affair is branded as adultery or otherwise disapproved of in adulthood. Its very forbiddenness then enhances its intensity and tenacity. Even as late as old age, it is possible to have another love affair. The shorter life expectancy of men, however, limits the supply of potential male partners for many of their widows.

Regardless of whether it is called love or infatuation, when a new affair in the life of one of the partners rocks the boat of an established relationship, then the navigation light of popular culture, in America and elsewhere, illuminates the platitude that love conquers all. According to one version of this platitude, if you fall in love with a new partner, all else must be sacrificed irrespective of the cost. As for the partner who is being abandoned, the navigation light of popular culture illuminates the green-eyed dragon of jealousy, litigation, alimony, and child custody, irrespective of personal penalties and self-sabotage.

The outcome differs, of course, in societies in which polygamy is legal, as in Islam, for instance, or in societies in which there is a long-standing tradition of keeping a concubine or a mistress. In American society, it is only the unconventional person, man or woman, who lives without acrimony as a partner in a threesome or foursome. There is no socially endorsed tradition for underwriting such an arrangement. In the sex therapy movement, for example, it is assumed virtually without exception that treatment is directed toward the couple, or the formation of a couple. Likewise it is virtually universal that explicit videos used for instruction in sex education or therapy presuppose a marital or otherwise bonded relationship between two people exclusively. By contrast, explicit videos made for erotic entertainment display various multiple and casual relationships, but not as serious solutions or alternatives to the breakup of a bonded couple's relationship.

The magnet of limerence that draws two people together is not universally of the same strength, but variable from one couple to another. One source of variability is the degree to which the lovemaps and gendermaps of the two people reciprocally match one another. When the match is nearer to being completely one-sided rather than reciprocal, then the situation that ensues is one of love partially or wholly unrequited. The person who one-sidedly and wrongly decodes the lovemap/gendermap of the other gets locked into the error, and then the lock freezes. He or she may then stalk the other person, becoming possibly homicidal and/or suicidal. This unilateral fixation on unrequited love goes by the name of Clérambault-Kandinsky syndrome, and is also known as erotomania.

Reciprocality: Career Compatibility

When the lovemap/gendermap match is partially, though not completely reciprocal, then the two people may proceed on the assumption that after a period of living together, the mismatches will be corrected. The correction process, however, becomes an adversarial power struggle which diminishes rather than increases reciprocality. Eventually the day of reckoning dawns, and one or each partner reaches the point of giving up on the possibility of reciprocality.

In a society in which the marriages of its young people are arranged by their elders, one may attribute a gendermap/lovemap mismatch to a mistake that might have been avoided had the young people been allowed more freedom of choice. It is not a foregone conclusion, however, that marriage by family arrangement produces gendermap or lovemap mismatching either more or less often than marriage by personal arrangement does. However, statistics may be unascertainable if marriages are arranged and separation or divorce is socially prohibited. In the United States, where marriages are mostly self-arranged and divorce is tolerated, the divorce rate hovers at around 50 percent, which suggests that self-arranged marriages have a 50:50 chance of being either well matched or mismatched. Self-matching is no guarantee against miscalculation and mistake. The mistake may represent a miscalculation of the extent of reciprocity in the specifications of each partner's gendermap, or if gendermap reciprocity presents no problem, then in the broader specifications of each partner's lovemap.

Mismatches may occur at many different locations on either the gendermap or lovemap. In the case of the gendermap, for example, mismatching trouble may occur, despite high sexuoerotic compatibility, if the two maps are incompatible with respect to career. The readout from his gendermap is, say, that his intramural (domestic) career is secondary, albeit by no means negligible, whereas his extramural career is primary and should be accorded priority over hers. The readout from her gendermap is that the ideal husband or lover is not only a virtuoso in bed, but also a top-level business manager who accords her extramural career so much priority that he guarantees her escalation to the summit, and concurrently minimizes the intrusions and distractions of domesticity. Those with sufficient income might come to a resolution by purchasing domestic help. Otherwise it becomes all but impossible for two people to resolve the incompatibility of the extramural career component of their two gendermaps equitably, without one yielding gendermap priority to the other.

Not invariably, though very often, career incompatibility then overtakes the sexuoerotic component of both gendermaps. Passion dies, and sexual intercourse becomes perfunctory or ceases. The two people live under the same roof and eat at the same table like guests in the same boarding house. This is a hazardous arrangement. At any time, the sparks of gendermap mismatching are likely to conflagrate so that reconciliation is not only unlikely, but impossible. When they do, the mismatched couple has only three possibilities. One is to do nothing except to maintain the highly unsatisfactory status quo. Another is to precipitate and maybe litigate a separation. A third is to engage in battle with tactics either of active aggression that may escalate to homicide, or of passive aggression that may escalate to suicide, or of joint homicide/suicide.

Maintaining the status quo is not necessarily to the advantage of either party. It can be as burdensome to carry the responsibility of amassing a fortune from an extramural career as it can be by not doing so and thereby forfeiting self-esteem and the autonomy of achievement. The career husband may neglect and deprive his wife and family; but the underachieved and ambitious wife may abuse his income and humiliate him for not outperforming his rivals, or for being inadequate in bed.

Maintaining the status quo is not necessarily stable and predictable. It may be interrupted by stress-induced or stress-facilitated breakdown of the functioning of the body. There are a great many such diagnoses of breakdown. The symptoms may be physical or mental, including chronic fatigue and depression. Breakdown of the body may be lethal, as in a stress-induced heart attack.

Like doing nothing, escaping from the dilemma of mismatching gendermaps is fraught also with hazard for both partners. Escape usually means separation or divorce, but not always. It may be achieved partially by working very late hours away from home, or working for long periods at distant locations.

There is also the escape of becoming symbolically another person. This happens in the dissociative syndrome of dual or multiple personality in which an incipient "alter" becomes activated. A rare but dramatic example of dual personality entails two names, two wardrobes, two personalities, and two careers, the original one male, and the secondary one female (or vice versa). In the male, the feminine personality appears in response to a precipitating stress and signifies a complete transposition of the gendermap's masculine and feminine schemas. Correspondingly, in women female and male gendermap schemas may interchange. If the two schemas alternate each may require an appropriate sexuoerotic partner, male or female, respectively, or else no sexuoerotic partner at all. In some cases the two schemas of the gendermap fail or cease to alternate, and the person becomes a full-time male-to-female or female-to-male transexual.

Another hazard is exploitation, often achieved with litigation and, for the wealthy, involving very large amounts of money or property. In some cases, an individual achieves power over another deviously by faking gendermap matching with a prearranged plan of blackmail or legal divorce involving a large settlement.

For couples who have children, another hazard is that parents and infants become pairbonded with a bond that does not yield to separation or divorce. For the children joint custody is the ideal, but without compromise there is no wholly satisfactory universal formula for joint custody. For the parent who has primary custody, the economic disadvantage of the single parent family may well outweigh the advantage of being unattached or divorced.

Engaging in battle when gendermaps mismatch is, like doing nothing or escaping, also hazardous for both partners. Fighting may be conducted as nagging and verbal harassment; it may be a devious undercover action or sabotage; it may be assaultive and violent; and it may be deadly. Active aggression is seldom misconstrued, whereas passive aggression is readily misconstrued as martyrdom and victimhood. Passive aggression may, however, be a devious way of instigating violence. The gendermap of a passive aggressive martyr, either male or female, may have its passivity augmented by dependency on either prescribed or illegal drugs, the most widely used of which is alcohol.

Two partners may engage each other in passive or in active aggression, or one may be actively and the other passively aggressive. If one partner, say the active aggressor, should reform and quit the actively aggressive role, then that role may be assumed by the other partner—and correspondingly for the passively aggressive role.

Once a mismatched gendermap battle gets under way, the precipitating cause of the war may remain unformulated in words and be entirely inchoate or, although once identified, completely lost sight of and displaced onto something different—not perfunctory sex, and not career issues, but red herrings and irrelevancies such as, say, vacation schedule, the PTA meeting, yard care, mother-in-law trouble, lack of understanding, being cold and unemotional, not communicating, and yelling at the children.

Reciprocality: Sexuoerotic Orientation

Reciprocal mismatching on the criterion of career, although potentially catastrophic for couples with dependent children or others in need of home care, may also be a major issue for couples without dependents. Reciprocal mismatching on the criterion of erotosexual orientation may affect any couple, whether of the same sex or mixed. In this erotosexual type of mismatching, it may be carelessly assumed that one of the partners must be homosexual and the other heterosexual, but that is an oversimplification. What usually occurs is that neither of the two partners is exclusively homosexual nor exclusively heterosexual in sexuoerotic orientation, but that both are somewhat bisexual, although not to the same degree. Many people take for granted that in the bisexual individual the homo:hetero ratio must be 50:50, which is actually quite rare. It is far more likely for the homo:hetero ratio to be off center—60:40, 30:70, 10:90, or some other combination.

Irrespective of whether they are same-sexed or different, if both partners of a bisexual couple have a homo:hetero ratio of 50:50, they are reciprocally matched. When the homo:hetero ratio deviates from exactly 50:50, reciprocal matching then requires that the ratio should be the same, irrespective of its magnitude, for both partners. Thus, in a mixed-sex couple, if the woman's homo:hetero ratio is 15:85 and the man's is 15:85 also, then both are predominantly heterosexual. In a same-sex couple, either two men or two women, the same 15:85 homo:hetero ratio would signify that both partners are only weakly homosexual. Between same sex couples, exact similarity of the homo:hetero ratio is less likely to be conducive to reciprocal matching of the lovemaps than is some degree of mutual difference in the homo:hetero ratio.

Mismatching of the homo:hetero ratio in a same-sex couple does not guarantee sexuoerotic compatibility. On the contrary, it may endanger it. Two men would not necessarily be compatibly matched, if for example one had a homo:hetero ratio of 100:0 (exclusively homosexual) and the other a ratio of 20:80 (predominantly heterosexual). Such a gay mismatch is not uncommon in the gay world, insofar as the lovemap of an exclusively homosexual man often specifies that the idealized lover should be a man who is ostensibly straight. The liaison between two such men is fragile and likely to be short-lived insofar as the predominantly heterosexual man is sexuoerotically more attracted to women than is his predominantly homosexual partner. The relationship may be based more on nonerotic expediency and exploitation than on sexuoerotic bonding. Exploitation may be for financial gain, better housing, social access to the rich and famous, career advancement, or whatever. Exactly the same applies to homo:hetero mismatching between two women or a man and a woman.

Far from being a deterrent, mismatching on the basis of the homo:hetero ratio, as in the foregoing example, might be a challenge for the exclusively homosexual partner, and one that would no doubt require many concessions to be made in the hope, probably in vain, of preserving the partnership. Similarly, homo:hetero ratio challenges apply also to attractions between men and women.

There is, for example, the predominantly or exclusively heterosexual woman who is fascinated by the filial attentiveness and uncoercive sexuoeroticism of a predominantly gay man. She herself may have what may be called a lady redeemer complex based on the popular stereotype of the power of love to conquer all. According to this stereotype, her love will enable her to remold his gendermap to fit the specifications of her own. The predominantly gay man responds to being remolded as if to being obedient to a mother or older sister. Then he gets married. Sexual intercourse with his wife is a perfunctory duty, but one that he performs for the sake of fatherhood. He is intensely attracted to the role of being a father and is very good at parenting. The frequency of intercourse progressively diminishes. The act itself is for him accompanied by mental imagery of having sex with someone else, a man. In secret he begins dating a man and having an affair with him. Eventually, of course, his wife finds out that he has not been remolded. The range of socially prescribed and acceptable responses to their dilemma is narrow: either continuing the status quo, engaging in battle, or following the prevalent social stereotype of getting separated and divorced. Young people are not prepared in advance with role models without being stigmatized, as in living together but each having an outside lover.

The foregoing scenario can be matched by one in which the man's homo:hetero ratio is predominantly heterosexual and that of the woman to whom he is attracted is predominantly lesbian. Close friendship with physical contact between women is not severely frowned upon, socially, so that a woman may be able to carry on an undisclosed lesbian affair for years before "coming out," and, perhaps, leaving her husband and grown children.

Paraphilic Lovemaps

There are many scenarios and personalized variations of gendermap mismatching on the basis of the homo:hetero ratio, as well as on the basis of career. In addition, both the mismatching or the matching of gendermaps may be compounded by the intrusion of paraphilic lovemap mismatching. A lovemap develops so as to be sexuoerotically coded as either normophilic, hypophilic, hyperphilic or paraphilic. The criteria of normophilia are not absolute but ideological and transculturally variable. Hypophilia signifies troublesome insufficiency or incompleteness of sexuoerotic arousal and genital function, up to and including orgasm. Hyperphilia signifies a vexatious excess of sexuoerotical arousal and genital function in either duration or frequency. Paraphilia signifies that sexuoerotical arousal and orgasmic climax are fixatedly contingent upon a rehearsal in imagery and ideation of eccentric or bizarre practices or rituals that may also be carried out in actual behavior. The formal definition of paraphilia is as follows.

> **paraphilia:** a condition occurring in men and women of being compulsively responsive to and obligatively and fixatedly dependent on an unusual and personally or socially unacceptable stimulus, perceived or in the ideation and imagery of fantasy, for optimal initiation and maintenance of erotosexual arousal and the facilitation or attainment of orgasm (from Greek, *para-*, altered + *-philia*). Paraphilic imagery may be replayed in fantasy during solo masturbation or intercourse with a partner. In legal terminology, a paraphilia is a perversion or deviancy; and in the vernacular it is kinky or bizarre sex.

Not enough is known about the concatenation of factors responsible for the shaping of a lovemap into a paraphilic one. Allowance must be made for a vulnerability or risk factor present in some but not all boys and girls. Boys with an extra Y chromosome (the 47, XYY syndrome), for example, have such a risk factor.

It is in the postnatal biography of paraphilias, however, that one looks for early evidence of the genesis of a paraphilic lovemap. There it is common to find early traumatization of the developing lovemap, particularly at around eight years of age. Any kind of traumatic suffering, including abusive neglect and injurious violence, nonsexual as well as sexual may be implicated. So also may exposure to sexual or erotic pursuits out of synchrony with the developmental sexological age. The most frequent traumatization, however, is from the quandary, popularly known as a Catch-22 (see chap. 6) of being damned if you do and damned if you don't confess to having eaten of the forbidden fruit, for example, by having obtained forbidden sexual knowledge, or by having been a participant in prohibited sexual activity, consensually or otherwise, as in childhood sexual rehearsal play. In either case, one is damned if the prohibited knowledge or activity is disclosed or discovered and, if they are not discovered, damned by the looming threat that they will be. The damnation is particularly onerous in the case of incest, for the sanctions of the taboo against it are so powerful and punitive.

The outcome of being caught in a Catch-22 may be, according to the opponent-process theory of Richard Solomon (Money, 1988b), that negative converts to positive. Otherwise stated, aversion converts to addiction, after which the individual repeats *ad infinitum* that which once was forbidden, prohibited, and punished, no matter how dangerous or self-sabotaging. This is the formula whereby a normophilic lovemap converts to a paraphilic one. Triumph is snatched from the jaws of tragedy, and carnal lust is preserved, but at the cost of its separation from affectional love.

Whether paraphilic or otherwise, a person's lovemap bears the stamp of individuality just as does his/her thumbprint. Lovemaps do, however, share certain generic characteristics that allow them to be classified by type. The number of lovemaps add up to around forty. The exact number varies according to cutoff point between types, subtypes, and combination or multiplex types. The full list with definitions is given in Money (1988a, 1988b). The forty-odd paraphilias exemplify seven grand stratagems by which carnal lust is preserved but at the cost of being separated from affectional love.

- The **sacrificial/expiatory stratagem** is typified by sadism and masochism which are manifested, respectively, at one extreme by serial lust murder, and conversely, at the other extreme, by accidental death from autoerotic asphyxiation.

- The marauding/predatory stratagem is typified by stalking and assaultative rape, or conversely by risking self-exposure to sexual assault.
- The mercantile/venal stratagem is typified by self-assignment to a career of being paid for sex as a female prostitute or male hustler, or conversely to a career of putting oneself in the position of being blackmailed or robbed.
- The fetishistic/talismanic stratagem is typified by performing sexually with, or with the aid of a fetishistic object or conversely by assisting a fetishistic partner. Fetishes belong in two categories, the touchy-feelies (hyphephilias) and the smelly-tasties (olfactophilias) both of which have phyletic origins in sensory stimuli from the human body.
- The stigmatic/eligibilic stratagem is typified by a self-originated restriction on the age (chronophilia) or body morphology (morphophilia) of the partner, or conversely of impersonating that same age and body morphology. An example of age specificity is having a juvenile partner (pedophilia) and conversely of impersonating a juvenile oneself. An example of morphophilia is paraphilic amputeeism, that is of having a partner with an amputated stump, and conversely of impersonating an amputee, or arranging self-amputation.
- The solicitational/allurative stratagem is typified by a fixation on genital exhibitionism and conversely a fixation on peeping or voyeurism.
- The subrogation/understudy stratagem is typified by becoming a substitute for someone else, as happens, for example, in those cases of incest in which a son or daughter rescues the mother from the obligation and disgust of having sex with her husband by becoming his partner in her place. The converse is typified in those cases of adultery in which having someone else's partner as a stand-in for one's own regular partner is essential to the excitement of sexual satisfaction.

Two people whose gendermaps are mismatched may be lovemap mismatched also, as for paraphilic sadomasochism, or for paraphilic exhibitionism/voyeurism, or for pedophilia/gerontophilia and so on. The latter is a rare and extreme example of agemap mismatching. Far more common is age mismatching in which the extremes are midlife or older and young adulthood. In such a case, the lovemap age of the older person has not kept in step with the advance of chronological age. The two partners of the same age who were well matched when younger become mismatched in midlife. Eventually, one of them (usually not both) becomes fixated on a much younger partner. This is the dynamic that lies behind the otherwise unexplained dissolution of many relationships, both gay and straight, married and unmarried. It may be construed as the fountain-of-youth mismatch.

Another example of a dynamic of lovemap mismatching that affects both gay and straight relationships pertains to paraphilic expiation, that is sacrifice and its obverse, martyrdom. Like all paraphilic dynamics, this one separates the spiritual purity of affectational love from the sin of carnal lust. It is a dynamic that requires reparation or atonement for the sin of carnal lust by way of penance and sacrifice. Atonement may be exacted from oneself as the martyr, or from the partner. Self-martyrdom is exemplified in, for example, paraphilic self-strangulation (asphyxiophilia) (Money et al., 1991), in which the attainment of orgasm is contingent on risking death as the outcome of a possible split-second failure to release the asphyxiating cord or binding. Sacrificing someone else as the paraphilic martyr is exemplified at the greatest extreme by killing the partner, which is what happens in paraphilic serial murder. At a lesser extreme, the martyr does not die but is sadistically humiliated and abused.

It cuts across the grain of common sense that the euphoric feeling that builds up to orgasm should become inexorably enchained to violence and abuse directed toward either the self or the sexuoerotic partner. Much of human behavior, however, lies beyond the bounds of intuitive common sense. Thus it is counterintuitive that expiatory paraphilic abuse could be consensually agreed upon. Nonetheless, it is well known that some people do consent to extreme degrees of sadomasochistic enslavement or martyrdom. These practices induce in them sexuoerotic euphoria (Keyes and Money, 1993).

It is counterintuitive also that a partner in a feuding and violently abusive relationship would, instead of escaping, not only remain in the relationship but, if rescued, would return for more. However, this phenomenon does, indeed, occur. The explanation is that human beings become addicted to abuse. Although it remains to be experimentally demonstrated, it is possible that addiction to abuse may be brought on by a flood of endorphin, the brain's own version of morphine. Endorphins are manufactured in brain cells, and may be released in response to injury. It is, therefore possible for the pain of injury to be transformed into endorphin-induced sexuoerotic euphoria.

Upon being reunited after a lengthy separation, a couple's first sexual intercourse is often spectacularly ecstatic. The same may apply to what has been called the reconciliation fuck following feuding or abuse. The abuser begs to be reinstated and swears that abuse it will not happen ever again. The spectacular reward of the reconciliation orgasm convinces the victim, if not the both of them, that love has returned, and that being in love conquers all, abuse included. Then the cycle repeats itself.

Regardless of the context in which they appear or the stimulus to which they are the response, feuding, violence, and abuse have their phylogenetic origins in the dominance hierarchy of group membership. Jockeying for position on the dominance ladder is typical among species, especially primates, that live in kinship groups. When gendermaps are mismatched for career or for orientation, or when lovemaps are paraphilically mismatched, couple feuding is, in the final analysis, feuding over who has the greater power to be top dog. The techniques of feuding, ranging from wily stratagems to brute force, employ aggression but are not caused by it.

To recapitulate what has already been stated, it is sometimes, though not invariably possible to effect a redistribution of power that defuses the feud. Alternatively, the feud may continue or escalate. Another possibility is that one party surrenders or quits, with or without arbitration. In the absence of satisfactory arbitration, feuding may continue deviously as sabotage. When children are caught in the crossfire of devious sabotage, the effects on them are devastating.

· 8 ·

Public Policy Mismatching

Career Liberation
Feuding Deviously
Pornography
Harassment
Lesbianism as a Political Statement
Disposable Males
Demonification of Lust
Epilogue

· 8 ·

Public Policy Mismatching

Career Liberation

I n the foregoing chapters, the account of what happens to couples when their gendermaps collide is, besides being clinically authentic, a parable of what has happened in American society and elsewhere during the second half of the twentieth century. This has been the era of the sexual revolution and of the backlash of the sexual counterrevolution.

When Betty Friedan launched the second wave of the feminist movement with *The Feminine Mystique* (1963), she perceived prophetically the conflict between women's two careers, the one at home and the other extramural. "She must create, out of her own needs and abilities," she wrote, "a new life plan, fitting in the love and children and home that have defined femininity in the past with the work toward a greater purpose that shapes the future" (p. 338). To this she added, "There are no easy answers in America today . . . each woman . . . must unequivocally say 'no' to the housewife image. This does not mean, of course, that she must divorce her husband, abandon her children, give up her home. She does not have to choose between marriage and career. . . . It is not difficult . . . to combine marriage and motherhood and even the kind of lifelong personal purpose that once was called 'career'" (p. 342).

Under careers, Friedan subsumed "the lifelong commitment to an art or science, to politics or profession," not to trades, assembly lines, or day laboring. Friedan addressed only the upper echelon of highly educated women, not the underclass of poverty and partial literacy, and she made the momentous mistake of not addressing also their men, so as to engage their reciprocity. Feminist philosophy regarding men was that women can do all that men can do—and more, namely, having an extramural career and running a home and family, too. That would prove to be hyperbole.

There was no methodology to guarantee that all women could be transformed so as to possess the revised feminist version of the gendermap, nor all men its masculine counterpart. At its outset, feminism would be enrolling the converted, and then recruiting missionaries to convert the heathen.

It is a matter of history that the new feminism did attract followers. Its message appealed to those whose family-plus-career gendermaps were already in place. It appealed also to women with a lesbian gendermap in which the possibility of sexual intercourse with a male was missing, whereas the possibility of a nondomestic career was in place. In addition, it appealed to gay men in whose gendermaps the possibility of sexual intercourse with a female was missing, whereas the possibility of domesticity despite an extramural, income-producing career was in place. Nongay men whose gendermaps were orthodoxly and traditionally imprinted rarely or never formed or joined profeminist organizations. Some traditional men were supportive of their feminist friends and relatives, but some were not, and likewise some traditionalist women were not. Some traditionalist women formed antifeminist organizations, for example, Phyllis Schlafly's Eagle Forum, and crusaded vigorously against equal rights for women and against sex education for juveniles and adolescents, but in favor of integrity of the idealized traditional white middle-class family. Their male counterparts bonded in paramilitary groups. A few traditionalist men eventually formed a men's movement and went off on male-bonding retreats to beat tom-toms, chant, and reclaim their caveman virility in the woods (Bly, 1990; Keen, 1991; Farrell, 1993).

In the 1960s, the mainstream feminist movement ran concurrently with the sexual revolution, but the two did not unite. Feminism was tolerant of women's sexual liberation, but its focus was not on sexuality and eroticism, per se, with or without the Pill or other forms of contraception, but on the compatibility of pregnancy and parenthood with an extramural career. Equality of career opportunity became defined as equality on the basis of gender. Sexuality and eroticism were taken for granted or prudishly set aside, which was possible since gender had replaced sex in the feminist lexicon. At this stage of their history, feminism and traditionalism were like the couple who neither separate nor fight, but simply stay together, tolerating the status quo. It was not to last that way.

Just as two individuals can part company to avoid fighting, that is a possibility with groups, also, but not when the two groups are the two halves of the human species, males and females. In science fiction one might envision a scenario in which males and females live in separate herds, meeting only seasonally to breed. Alternatively one may envision a scenario, borrowed from animal husbandry, of the stud farm where males are culled from the herd, except for a few prized breeding specimens (see chap. 5). This could be called the harem scenario, provided the few prized males were in charge. If the stud farm was ruled by women, however, then it would be called the amazon scenario. Either way, it does not eradicate the dilemma of who has the power of dominance, men over women, or women over men. A scenario in which females are culled from the herd, leaving only a select few for breeding, would be feasible only as a desperate measure of population decrease.

Human beings have done enough weird things in the course of history that anything envisioned in science fiction cannot be totally ruled out as becoming an actuality. However, to all intents and purposes, mass segregation of males or females can be dismissed as impossible. The sociobiological principle of individual sexuoerotic attraction and pairbonding is so powerful that it would override a policy of universal mass segregation of the sexes.

Feuding Deviously

When toleration of the status quo does not succeed, and when separation is not an option, the alternative for organizations, as for couples, is to feud. Whereas the mainstream organization of feminism followed the strategies of political and judicial opposition, affiliated factions and individuals, frustrated by slow progress and defeat, especially the defeat of the Equal Rights Amendment in 1982, adopted a different strategy. They were more overtly adversarial but, like all underdogs unable to match the power of the enemy, they had no alternative but to resort to deviousness. Their deviousness derived from the separation of lust-free gender from lust-filled sexuality. Their enemy was men, and their target was men's lust. It could hardly have been men's gender, since gender equality of career rights was the source of the struggle.

An early sign of the change in strategy was the publication in 1975 of Susan Brownmiller's *Against Our Will*. This book paved the way for dogmas that have already been mentioned, namely, that rape is an act not of sexuality but ostensibly of violence; that men equate sexual intercourse with the assertion of power over women; that women are the victims of sexuality and men the perpetrators; and, among extremists, even that every act of sexual intercourse is itself an act of rape. It paved the way also for the social construction and naming of two new offenses, date rape and marital rape, as well as for legal sanctions against them, and for the funding of rape crisis centers for the treatment of victims. The battered wife syndrome received more attention, also, but not with the same media prominence as rape.

Much the same occurred with the battered child syndrome. It received diminishing attention as public and media interest grew in the sexual abuse and molestation of children by strangers, family members or friends, and in the school or the church. A new legal industry grew in defense of adult victims who recalled sexual abuse three or four decades earlier, for whom the statute of limitations was changed so that it was timed from the date of first recall in adulthood. It became common for recall to be factitious, and to have been precipitated by therapists and self-styled specialists of whom too many have dubious credentials and are unlicensed.

Another new industry for the ostensible prevention of childhood sexual abuse grew in education. Curricula were developed for kindergarten and all grades. They have not been adequately tested for validity and efficacy, and are open to the suspicion of doing more harm than good by traumatizing children (Krivacska, 1990). They are evasive about the genital organs, their names, and their functions, and use instead such terms as *good touch* and *bad touch*.

The foregoing developments were to some degree influenced by factions within the feminist movement, though in the larger context and more amorphous social policy of the counterreformation. The same influences apply to the issue of pornography.

Pornography

Attacking men by attacking pornography (see chaps. 4 and 5) is a dirty little war by way of either malicious intent or sexological naiveté. It is a war that completely bypasses women's pornography. In the case of men's pornography, it fails to differentiate the pornography of deviance (paraphilia) from the pornography of normalcy.

Women's pornography is as plentiful as men's, but in today's market it is found in magazines and paperbacks more than in the visual media. It is not prosecuted as illegal, because it does not depict external genitalia in action, nor describe them in explicit detail. It is attentive to the romantic narrative story line. In keeping with female sexuality and eroticism, its imagery is predominantly tactual rather than visual, and of being swept away by passion.

One of the sex-shared/threshold-dimorphisms of chapter 2 is that men as compared with women are less dependent on the tactual than the visual sense to be turned on sexually and erotically. Even in narrative pornography for men, the imagery is visual rather than tactual, as it is also in the erotic dreams (wet dreams) of pubertal and adolescent boys and men. Males who are not visually turned on, which is the case in some genetic and endocrine syndromes, are turned on either minimally or not at all. Visual turn-on is perceptual, as for example, by the visual appearance of a girlfriend or wife, as well as by the imagery of dreams and reveries, or of imagery portrayed in the print or electronic media.

There are no statistics that reveal the proportion of males who are normophilically versus paraphilically turned on. Even though our society is singularly successful in raising children to have vandalized gendermaps, it is probable that the majority of males have gendermaps that have not been rendered vandalized. Males pairbond as do females. They fall in love. They become love stricken. They do not perceive the partner as nothing more than a sex object or toy. They do not depersonalize her. They do not, with Foucault and his feminist adherents, socially construct all sexual encounters into maneuvers of power and dominance. They are not all sexual sadists or rapists. Men are not pornography-driven skeletal structures attached to a penis as they are portrayed in the outpourings of contemporary writers like, for example, Andrea Dworkin (1979/1989), and the legal scholar Catherine MacKinnon (1987, chap. 4; 1993).

Pornography is not caught by social contagion from the printed page or video. If a pornographic depiction does not match your own particular gendermap and lovemap, then it will not appeal to you but leave you indifferent or disgusted. If it were otherwise, hours of viewing heterosexual pornography would convert homosexuality to heterosexuality, and vice versa, but that is not the case.

Feminists who attack pornography fall into a trap set by their antifeminist opponents, for they offer proof that women are morally too fragile to share sexuality and eroticism on an equal, although reciprocal basis with men, and therefore must be legislatively, legally, and personally protected. That turns the clock backwards and puts women in the position of being subordinate to men who have more power over them than they have over men.

Not all feminists are against pornography (Tisdale, 1992; Pally, 1994); witness the organization of Feminists for Free Expression. Increasingly women have recognized that censorship of pornography endangers all explicitly sexual publications, including those published by feminists themselves, and they have seen it actually happen in Canada. In February 1992, the Supreme Court in Ottawa made a ruling on pornography based on MacKinnon's argument that pornography is harmful to women by degrading and dehumanizing them. In response to the danger and misuse of this ruling, a group of women feminists have joined forces with other organizations and formed the National Coalition Against Censorship and published a pamphlet, *The Sex Panic: Women, Censorship, and "Pornography"* (1993).

Harassment

The dilemma of pornography is also the dilemma of sexual harassment in the workplace. Regulations to protect women in the workplace are regulations to protect women from men not from other women. Women protected from men are not accorded equal status with men. Instead, their status is that of being potential victims who should avoid harassment either by staying at home or by being reliant on the guardianship of a presumably powerful male.

Harassment is not gender specific, nor is it specifically sexual. The younger, smaller, and weaker in society have always needed the protection of the stronger. Every schoolchild knows that. Feminism made a tactical error by allowing harassment in the workplace to be qualified as sexual, instead of being generic. Specifying it as sexual, and omitting lesbian harassment, marked it as part of the devious campaign against men by attacking male flirtation, sexuality, and eroticism, in its normal as well as its pathological expression.

This sort of attack spread beyond harassment in the workplace and beyond feminism to be taken up as media harassment of public figures, including presidential candidate Bill Clinton in 1991, as a maneuver for morally discrediting them. This maneuver is another example of feminist and counterreformation policies in chronological, though not necessarily causal coexistence.

Although it was presumably unplanned, the feminist attack on male sexuality combined with the counterreformation attack on sexuality in general provided the media with an unparalleled opportunity to provide the public with live hearings and detailed reports that featured explicit sexual vocabulary and explicit accounts of sexual practices that formerly would have been censored. For example, in 1990 the nation as well as much of the world was glued to its television screens while Anita Hill and Clarence Thomas, in the Senate hearings for Thomas's appointment to the Supreme Court, each gave specific sexual details of what had been construed to be sexual harassment of her by him when they formerly worked together.

In 1991 there was a similar fascination with minutiae of rape in the trial in Palm Beach, Florida, of William Kennedy Smith, nephew of Senator Edward Kennedy, who had been present at the Kennedy mansion on the night of the alleged incident.

From December 1993 to January 1994, an estimated sixty million people with cable television followed the trials of John and Lorena Bobbitt. The public was provided with detailed revelations of alleged rape, anal sex, lack of orgasm, and the culminating act in which the wife cut off her husband's penis with a kitchen knife and threw it from her car into an empty lot from which it was retrieved and reattached surgically. There were televised inquiries also about regeneration of function and erotic feeling. Although there was still no book in English with the word penis in the title, during the Bobbitt trial this once suppressed word was heard in network television newscasts in every household hundreds of times, if not more often.

The editors and writers of tabloid newspapers have known for a couple of centuries or more that sexual information prohibited as such can be reported with the appropriate sounds of moral disapproval as police-blotter or courtroom gossip. This is the principle of having your cake and eating it too. Today's equivalent are television's talk shows and news tabloids. They have capitalized on what feminism and the counterreformation have disapproved of as sexually harassing or deviant practices, some of them paraphilic and bizarre, by getting guests who are either their victims or their exponents to reveal all in person. In this topsy turvy way, the sexual revolution is, in part, kept alive by even its opponents. Through television, more people know more about sex and sexological pathology than ever before in history.

Lesbianism as a Political Statement

A manifestation of antimale partisanship within the feminist movement was the emergence, during the period that straddled the seventies and eighties, of the doctrine that lesbianism is a political statement against men. According to this doctrine, lesbianism is a voluntary choice, not a sexual orientation. The idea that both homosexuality and heterosexuality, male or female, are voluntary sexual preferences was popular at the time, as it still is amongst social constructionists. Lesbianism as political statement failed to gain a substantial following. The wonder is that it was ever expected to do so. One possible explanation may be sought in women's greater dependence on tactual than visual stimuli for sexuoerotic arousal. Without the prerequisite necessity of having to see the partner, it may be more readily possible to be aroused tactually by a partner of either sex. In that case, it would be bisexualism, not lesbianism that might constitute a political statement. Be that as it may, the pull of monosexual attraction toward men is for the majority of women stronger than bisexual attraction toward women as well as men. For a minority, monosexual attraction toward women, or one particular woman, is stronger. In some lesbian partnerships that begin after early adulthood, one or both women already have one or more offspring whom they rear together.

Disposable Males

Some childless lesbian couples, having decided on parenthood, need a male only for his semen, delivered if not in person, then by artificial insemination. For them the male, his function fulfilled, becomes a completely disposable sex object. The disposable man is in demand also for heterosexual women who circumvent the competing demands of husband and career by opting for single parenthood.

Male disposability may be partial rather than complete. Some women entertain their children's father as a night guest on a part-time basis only. They do not tolerate his presence on a full-time basis.

The problems of incompatibility between couples continue to be reducible, aphoristically, to either sex or the checkbook, and when either collapses so also does the relationship. The divorce rate continues to hover at around 50 percent. When couples separate, the mother more often than the father claims the children, or is left with them. When the father does not support his children financially, if the family system is three-generational, the grandparents may come to the rescue. Otherwise the mother either goes to work, finds new male support, or obtains welfare assistance. Single-parent fathers are not given much credence by society. Nor do they get welfare support by the state. The children of single-parent welfare mothers are being threatened by withdrawal of state financial assistance so as to force the mother to go to work. All too often, however, no jobs are available. For these women the feminist cure of an extramural career as well as family life is laced with poison. Those whom the feminist ideal has not served well are in the economically and educationally less privileged echelons of society.

Among women whom feminism serves well are those who circumvent the conflict between household and extramural careers in favor of the latter. Some are women who live alone without a full-time partner. Some share a household jointly with a companion, and some employ a retainer. Some are childless, either by plan or as a consequence of unplanned infertility. Among those who have children, feminism serves well also those whose incomes or joint incomes allow the employment of domestic help, and those whose conjugal partners reciprocate the duality of their careers.

Feminism has not yet found a solution for those women who, once they become mothers, are so fully occupied by the demands of home that they interrupt their extramural career either temporarily or long-term. The penalties of not being able to catch up following a career interruption, whatever the reason, may be severe and insurmountable, not only for women, but for men also. The interruption penalizes also those supervisors who have invested in career training for the trainee who becomes a dropout, as well as those colleagues who must cover for the temporary absences of workmates due to the exigencies of family and childcare.

Demonification of Lust

Subverting its achievements in advancing equal rights for women outside the home, the feminist movement made a tactical error in changing the battle over equal career rights into a battle over men's sexuality. There is an aphorism that warns one not to engage in a battle that can't be won. There is no chance of winning concessions from men for an equal share of their long established political, economic, legal, and vocational power by attacking their masculine sexuality and lust—and even less of a chance when concurrently failing to differentiate pathological from normal lust, and erroneously equating the sexuality and lust of all men with pathology. This is like an attack on colonial oppressors. It can be won only by exterminating the oppressors or driving them away. Not all men are like colonial oppressors, however, and not all women perceive men that way. These men and women are bewildered by the virulence of the attack, by the backlash of contempt for women that it provokes, and by the distrust that it foments between the male and female members of a species that lives together in pairs and in groups.

Feminist rhetoric will not be able to destroy the phyletically ordained pairbonding and troopbonding of our species, but it may be able to undermine the trust that men and women have in one another, without which the sharing of equal rights will be forever doomed.

From this none too optimistic vantage point, it is evident that the feminist dilemma of extramural career versus children and home is part of the dilemma of gender versus sex in which sex encompasses eroticism and lust. It is a dilemma that has existed in moral philosophy for centuries. It is the dilemma of the Manichean heresy of the Prince of Light versus the Prince of Darkness, of love as spiritual, versus love as carnal and lustful. Gender is above the belt and pure. Sex and lust are below the belt, impure, obscene, and pornographic.

In postmodern social constructionist theory, which includes feminist theory, gender is socially constructed so as to be a neutered version of sex, and lust is socially constructed so as to be, in women, a spiritualized version of sex, and in men a demonized version.

Social constructionism is not a scientific movement, but a philosophical and literary one. Its sexual pronouncements represent sexosophy, the philosophy of sex, not sexology, the science of sex (Money, 1986, chaps. 4 and 5). Sexosophy belongs to ideology. Sexology belongs to science. Sexosophy and sexology do not mix. That is something of which today's social constructionist scholars are not aware. Let not either one be mistaken for the other. In the future, that will be to the benefit of us all.

Epilogue

It is possible for a paraphilia that is classified as deviant in one society to be institutionalized as ideologically acceptable in another. For example, in Western, but not in Islamic advertising, it is ideologically acceptable to depict models in lingerie and for viewers to be fetishistically aroused by the undergarments on the model. By contrast, the depiction of a naked woman would be condemned as pornographic. Another example, forbidden in the West but formerly fashionable in China, is the paraphilia for tiny feet, deformed by binding, and known as the golden lotus. This paraphilia served also as a strategy of social control. It subordinated footbound women of the upper class to permanent dependence on wealthy fathers, husbands, or pimps. It also required less wealthy men to work harder and earn more to gain access, if possible, to a prostitute with bound feet with which to satisfy their paraphilia. In the West, the counterpart of bound feet are the stiletto heels on the shoes of a dominatrix who uses them as weapons on wealthy customers. They pay handsomely for the masochistic privilege of being jabbed. The fetishistic attraction of high heels on women's street shoes is socially so completely acceptable that they are not defined as fetishes.

Understanding gendermaps and lovemaps, with and without paraphilias, is integral to understanding the sexology of not only the individual, but also of the society in which that individual lives. To understand the politics and sociology of any society, one must understand also the ideological sexology, better named the sexosophy of that society, as manifested in the gendermaps and lovemaps that it selectively endorses or rejects.

For a fuller understanding of America today, one must know that in the politics of sexual rights the gendermap is drawn as if by the makers of Ken and Barbie dolls (see chap. 4). Although plentifully endowed with sexual characteristics, these are dolls that have nothing sexual between their legs. Their gendermaps, like the gendermaps of American public policy, have been genitoerotically neutered. Genital sexuality and eroticism in American public policy have been confined within the lovemap and banned from explicit discussion in polite and official conversation. Discussion of the varied genital contents of the lovemap finds its way into the public forum not straightforwardly, but circuitously and deviously, as by the time-honored method of self-righteous media reports of gossip, blackmail, sex-crime trials, and confessions. Television soap operas and talk shows walk the tightrope of censorship, the outcome being salacious rather than salubrious. Sexually explicit videos, magazines, and computer bulletin boards test the limits of censorship and run afoul of the law. So also does sex on the Internet.

Discordance between morally cleansed and neutered gendermaps, on the one hand, and morally dirty and sexuoerotic lovemaps, on the other, filters down from public policy to children through the family, school, and church. The ultimate effect on children is to dirtify their own developing gendermaps and lovemaps. Epidemiologically that means an exponential increase in the prevalence of paraphilic lovemaps, generation by generation. A lovemap pathologized by paraphilia combined with a neutered gendermap carries a guarantee of being a bad omen for gender equality between men and women. Gender without genital sex and eroticism is a disaster for individuals. It is also a disaster for society about to enter the twenty-first century.

Appendix

Press Release from The Johns Hopkins Medical
Institutions, November 21, 1966, Announcing
the Establishment of the Gender Identity
Clinic for Transexuals

A Gender Identity Clinic to deal with the problems of the transexual, physically normal people who are psychologically the opposite sex, has been established at The Johns Hopkins Medical Institutions. Dr. Hoopes, as chairman of the Gender Identity Clinic staff, serves as spokesman for the group, which includes: Dr. Dietrich P. Blumer, assistant professor of psychiatry; Dr. Milton T. Edgerton, professor and plastic-surgeon-in-charge at Johns Hopkins; Dr. Howard W. Jones, Jr., associate professor of gynecology and obstetrics; Dr. Norman J. Knorr, assistant professor of psychiatry and plastic surgery; Dr. Claude J. Migeon, associate professor of pediatrics; Dr. John W. Money, associate professor of medical psychology and pediatrics; Dr. Eugene Meyer, professor of psychiatry; Dr. Horst K. Schirmer, associate professor of urology; and Mr. C. Frank Velkas, a psychologist and associate of Dr. Money.

Dr. John Money has long been an outstanding psychologist engaged in pioneering studies on the transexual patients seen at Hopkins. His interest encouraged Dr. Jones and Dr. Edgerton to undertake surgical treatment on some of these early patients. These experiences convinced both that a definitive study should be initiated. Dr. Edgerton then asked Dr. Hoopes to establish the Gender Identity Clinic. Dr. Hoopes said that it was only after much study and soul-searching that the full team was assembled and they embarked upon the project: "After exhaustively reviewing the available literature and discussing the problem with people knowledgeable in this area, I arrived at the unavoidable conclusion that these people need and deserve help." He said that the staff, proper to accepting its first patient, studied the problem in all of its dimensions: scientific, ethical, religious, and legal.

Dr. John E. Hoopes, the assistant professor of plastic surgery and chairman of the clinic staff, said the Gender Identity group has been in operation for one year. The staff has seen a few dozen patients, has completed surgery to change the external manifestations of sex in a small number of patients, and has initiated the surgical procedures in several additional patients. The clinic staff has limited itself to accepting two patients a month for initial evaluation. Many have been referrals from The Harry Benjamin Foundation of New York. The leader and namesake of this organization, a physician, has worked with transexuals for many years and is the author of a medical book on the subject: *The Transsexual Phenomenon*. The Benjamin Foundation was endowed by the Erickson Educational Foundation, which also is the sole source of research support for the Hopkins endeavor. Aside from the Foundation's patients, there have been requests for surgery from more than one hundred other individuals who have heard of the clinic.

Dr. Hoopes emphasized, "This program, including the surgery, is investigational. The transexual has never previously been given adequate medical attention. The most important result of our efforts will be to determine precisely what constitutes a transexual and what makes him remain that way. Medicine needs a sound means of alleviating the problems of gender identification and of fostering public understanding of these extremely unfortunate individuals. It is too early in the program to be either optimistic or pessimistic. We are still in the process of collecting accurate observations on the results of treatment."

A transexual is normal physically and biologically, at least in so far as can be determined at present; but he feels, behaves, and dresses as if he were of the opposite sex. Most transsexuals begin to show signs of their problem at age four or five; usually, for example, they have no interest in the childhood play activities of their sex. They often make the change in type of dress and social presentation while in high school or shortly thereafter. Far from living lives in the shadows of society, some of them, at least, after assuming their new identities graduate from college and go on to become successful in business or other endeavors. "Our patients are not psychotic but do have extreme adjustment difficulties because of their problem; they feel that nature has somehow gone awry, almost as if their mind is in the wrong body," Dr. Hoopes said. "You would probably never recognize a transexual as such if you met him casually, or even if you knew him well. I cannot state too emphatically how completely these people assume the role of the opposite sex. The male transexual looks, dresses, and acts exactly like a woman, and the same is true for his female counterpart. They are not simply transvestites, people who receive pleasure from just wearing the clothing of the opposite sex; nor are they homosexuals, as commonly defined." An overwhelming majority of transexuals are men, and so have been most of the clinic's patients. All races are affected. How many transsexuals are there in this country? Dr. Hoopes said, "There is no way to get at the exact number, but at the minimum there are thousands."

"Over the years, psychiatrists have tried repeatedly to treat these people without surgery, and the conclusion is inescapable that psychotherapy has not so far solved the problem. The patients have no motivation for psychotherapy and do not want to change back to their biological sex. The high incidence of suicide and self-mutilation among these people testifies to the magnitude of the problem. If the mind cannot be changed to fit the body, then perhaps we should consider changing the body to fit the mind."

The clinic staff meets once each month. A four-step process for screening, evaluating, treating, and following the patients has been established:

Step 1: The potential patient is first thoroughly interviewed, tested, and evaluated by a psychiatrist, a psychologist, and the surgeons. The clinic accepts only the nonpsychotic transexual, the patient whose major apparent anxiety is the haunting fear that he will be discovered. Family and personal histories are being collected and studied meticulously. Scores of examination techniques are being employed. "Many of these studies may prove to be blind alleys," Dr. Hoopes said, "but we wish to find out as much as possible about these people and how to help them. There is no known common denominator among transexuals, so we are looking for one." The findings are presented to the entire staff for a decision as to whether the outlook is sufficiently optimistic to accept the person as a patient and enter him into phase two of the study.

Step 2: More psychiatric testing is complete. Endocrine and other metabolic and chromosomal studies are begun. A trial of hormone therapy to effect body changes toward the desired masculine or feminine direction is an important aspect of Step 2. Advancement of the patient to phase three requires another decision by the staff on the basis of the additional data.

Step 3: A surgery team skilled in plastic, gynecologic, and urologic techniques performs an operation, or series of operations, to transform the patient's external sex organs into those of the desired sex.

Step 4: The patient is followed by the staff for an indefinite period of time, probably for the remainder of his life, coming back periodically for study, evaluation, and, if necessary, further treatment. His total adjustment and contribution to society are major yardsticks of the value of treatment. "Step 4 is probably the most important phase of the entire program," Dr. Hoopes said. "It is at this stage that we will measure our success or failure, that is: are these people happier and more useful citizens following surgery and other therapy than they were before?"

"I want it clearly understood," he added, "that I and the other members of the clinic committee must be very circumspect in public discussion of our activities. Anonymity must be preserved for our patients. Anything else not only would be improper, but it would be inimincal to the patients' welfare. These patients wish only to try to build new, happier lives for themselves after leaving Johns Hopkins. The staff, however, decided that I should discuss the problem of transexuality and the efforts of the clinic in an effort to gain some public understanding and sympathy for the problems of the transexual and for what we are trying to achieve."

Bibliography

Acton, W. 1875. *The Functions and Disorders of the Reproductive Organs in Childhood, Youth, Adult Age, and Advanced Age, Considered in Their Physiological, Social, and Moral Relations*. 6th ed. Philadelphia: Presley Blakiston.

American Heritage Dictionary. 1992. 3d ed. New York: Houghton and Mifflin.

Allen, L.S., and Gorski, R.A. 1992. Sexual orientation and the size of the anterior commissure in the human brain. *Proceedings of the National Academy of Sciences USA*, 89:7199-202.

Attorney General's Commission on Pornography. 1986. *Final Report*. Washington, D.C.: Government Printing Office.

Ayer, A.J. 1950. *Language, Truth and Logic*, 2d ed. London: V. Gollancz.

Bosinski, H.A.G.; Schubert, F.; Wille, R.; Heller, M.; and Arndt, R. 1994. MRI of corpus callosum and neuropsychological functions in female-to-male transsexuals. Poster presented at the 20th Annual Meeting of the International Academy of Sex Research, Edinburgh, U.K., June 28–July 3, 1994.

Boswell, J. 1980. *Christianity, Social Tolerance, and Homosexuality*. Chicago: University of Chicago Press.

de Beauvoir, S. 1952. *The Second Sex*. New York: Alfred A. Knopf.

Bly, R. 1990. *Iron John*. New York: Addison-Wesley.

Breuer, J., and Freud, S. 1895. *Studien über Hysterie*. Leipzig and Vienna: Franz Deuticke.

Brown, D.E. 1991. *Human Universals*. Philadelphia: Temple University Press.

Brownmiller, S. 1975. *Against Our Will: Men, Women and Rape*. New York: Simon and Schuster.

Chan, S.T.H. 1977. Spontaneous sex reversal in fishes. In *Handbook of Sexology*, ed. J. Money and H. Musaph. Amsterdam: Elsevier.

Comfort, A. 1963. *Sex in Society*. London: Duckworth.

Commission on Obscenity and Pornography. 1970. *The Report of the Commission on Obscenity and Pornography*. New York: Random House.

Derrida, J. 1967/1970. *Of Grammatology*, trans. G.C. Spivak [*De la Grammatologie*. Paris: Editions de Minuit, 1967]. Baltimore: Johns Hopkins University Press.

————. 1967/1978. *Writing and Difference*, trans. A. Bass [*L'Ecriture et la Difference*. Paris: Editions du Seuil, 1967]. Chicago: University of Chicago Press.

Dunn, K. 1994. Truth abuse. *The New Republic*, no. 4150:16–18, August 10.

Dworkin, A. 1979/1989. *Pornography: Men Possessing Women*. New York: Perigee, 1979. [Paperback, New York: E.P. Dutton, 1989.]

————. 1987. *Intercourse*. New York: Free Press.

Eberle, P., and Eberle, S. 1986. *The Politics of Child Abuse*. Seacaucus, N.J.: Lyle Stuart.

Eibl-Eibesfeldt, I. 1972. *Love and Hate: The Natural History of Behavior Patterns*. New York: Holt, Rinehart, and Winston.

Farabollini, F.; Hole, D.R.; and Wilson, C.A. 1988. Behavioral effects in adulthood of serotonin depletion by p-chlorophenylalanine given neonatally to male rats. *International Journal of Neuroscience*, 41:187–99.

Farrell, W. 1993. *The Myth of Male Power: Why Men Are the Disposable Sex*. New York: Simon and Schuster.

Foucault, M. 1978. *The History of Sexuality, Vol. I: An Introduction*, trans. R. Hurley. New York: Random House.

————. 1961/1965. *Madness and Civilization: A History of Insanity in the Age of Reason*, trans. R. Howard [*Histoire de la Folie*. Paris, Librairie Plon, 1961). New York, Random House.

————. 1963/1973. *The Birth of the Clinic; An Archaeology of Medical Perception*. [*Naissance de la Clinique; Une Archeologie du Regard Medical*. Paris: Presses Universitaires de France, 1963]. New York: Pantheon.

Friedan, B. 1963. *The Feminine Mystique*. New York: W.W. Norton.

————. 1994. *Newsweek*, 123(1):37.

Frydman, R.; Parneix, I.; Fries, N.; Testart, J.; Raymond, J.-P.; and Bouchard, P. 1988. Pregnancy in a 46, XY patient. *Fertility and Sterility*, 50:813–14.

Gagnon, J. 1974. *Human Sexualities*. Glenview, Ill.: Scott Foresman.
—— and Simon, W. 1973. *Sexual Conduct: The Social Sources of Human Sexuality*. Chicago: Aldine.
Gerall, A.A.; Moltz, H.; and Ward, I.L. 1992. *Handbook of Behavioral Neurobiology, Volume 11 Sexual Differentiation*. New York: Plenum Press.
Goffman, E. 1961. *Asylums: Essays on the Social Situation of Mental Patients and Other Inmates*. New York: Doubleday.
——. 1963. *Stigma: Notes on the Management of Spoiled Identity*. Englewood Cliffs, N.J.: Prentice-Hall.
Halberstam, D. 1993. Discovering sex. *American Heritage*, 44(3):39–58.
Halpern, D.F. 1992. *Sex Differences in Cognitive Abilities*. 2d ed. Hillsdale, N.J.: Lawrence Erlbaum Associates.
Hamer, D.H.; Hu, S.; Magnuson, V.L.; Hu, N.; and Pattatucci, A.M.L. 1993. A linkage between DNA markers on the X chromosome and male sexual orientation. *Science*, 261:321–27.
Hampson, J.G. 1955. Hermaphroditic appearance, rearing and eroticism in hyperàdrenocorticism. *Bulletin of the Johns Hopkins Hospital*, 96:265–73.
Handa, R.J.; Hines, M.; Schoonmaker, J.N.; Shryne, J.E.; and Gorski, R.A. 1986. Evidence that serotonin is involved in the sexually dimorphic development of the preoptic area in the rat brain. *Developmental Brain Research*, 30:278–82.
Heidegger, M. 1927/1962. *Being and Time*. [*Sein und Zeit*, Halle, 1927]. New York: Harper.
Hooker, E.A. 1957. The adjustment of the male overt homosexual. *Journal of Projective Techniques*, 21:17–31.
——. 1958. Male homosexuality in the Rorschach. *Journal of Projective Techniques*, 22:33–54.
Hooper, C. 1992. Biology, brain architecture, and human sexuality. *Journal of NIH Research*, 4(10):53–59.
Houtsmuller, E.J.; Brand, T.; de Jonge, F.H.; Joosten, R.; van de Poll, N.E.; and Slob, A.K. 1993. SDN-POA volume, sexual behavior and partner preference of male rats affected by perinatal treatment with ATD. Chapter 7 (Part 2) in E.J. Houtsmuller, *Prenatal Uterine Environment and Sexual Differentiation of Rats*, Ph.D. Dissertation, Erasmus Universiteit, Rotterdam, Netherlands.
Husserl, E. 1900–01/1970. *Logical Investigations*. [*Logische Untersuchungen*. Halle: S.M. Niemeyer, 1900–1901]. New York: Humanities Press.

Illich, I. 1976. *Medical Nemesis: The Expropriation of Health*. New York: Pantheon.

Jackson, P.; Barrowclough, I.W.; France, I.T.; and Phillips, L.I. 1980. A successful pregnancy following total hysterectomy. *British Journal of Obstetrics and Gynaecology*, 87:353–55.

Keen, S. 1991. *Fire in the Belly*. New York: Bantam.

Kempe, C.H.; Silverman, F.N.; Steele, B.F.; Droegemuller, W.; and Silver, H.K. 1980. The battered-child syndrome. In *Traumatic Abuse and Neglect of Children at Home*, ed. G.J. Williams and J. Money. Baltimore: Johns Hopkins University Press.

Kennedy, H. 1988. *Ulrichs: The Life and Works of Karl Heinrich Ulrichs, Pioneer of the Modern Gay Movement*. Boston: Alyson Publications.

Keyes, R.W., and Money, J. 1993. *The Armed Robbery Orgasm: A Lovemap Autobiography of Masochism*. Buffalo: Prometheus Books.

Krivacska, J.J. 1990. *Designing Child Sexual Abuse Prevention Programs: Current Approaches and a Proposal for the Prevention, Reduction, and Identification of Sexual Misuse*. Springfield, Ill.: Charles C Thomas.

Lacan, J. 1982. *Feminine Sexuality*. New York: W.W. Norton.

Laing, R.D. 1961. *The Self and Others*. London: Tavistock Publications.

———. 1967. *The Politics of Experience*. New York: Ballantine.

Leifer, R. 1990. Introduction: The medical model as the ideology of the therapeutic state. *The Journal of Mind and Behavior*, 11(3–4):247–58.

LeVay, S. 1991. A difference in hypothalamic structure between heterosexual and homosexual men. *Science*, 253:1034–37.

———. 1993. *The Sexual Brain*. Cambridge, Mass.: MIT Press.

Liebowitz, M.R. 1987. *The Chemistry of Love*. Boston: Little, Brown

Lorenz, K.Z. 1952. *King Solomon's Ring*. New York: Crowell.

MacKinnon, C.A. 1987. A feminist/political approach: "Pleasure under patriarchy." In *Theories of Human Sexuality*, ed. J.H. Geer and W.T. O'Donohue. New York: Plenum Press.

———. 1993. *Only Words*. Cambridge, Mass.: Harvard University Press.

Mahood J., and Wenberg, K. 1980. *The Mosher Survey: Sexual Attitudes of Forty-Five Victorian Women*. New York: Arno Press.

Masson, J.M. 1985. *The Assault on Truth: Freud's Suppression of the Seduction Theory*. New York: Penguin Books.

Mathur, A.K., and Joshi, A. 1994. Variation in the expression of sexual behaviour of rams under different rearing conditions. In *3d Asian Conference of Sexology Abstracts*, ed. R. Shah and V. Kulkarni. New Delhi, India.

Mathur, A.K.; Joshi, A.; and Khuswaha, B.P. 1994. Influence of intro-
ducing tubectomized ewes in expression of sexual behaviour of rams
reared in unisexual flock. In *3d Asian Conference of Sexology Abstracts*, ed. R. Shah and V. Kulkarni. New Delhi, India.

Mellon, S. 1994. Neurosteroids: Biochemistry, modes of action, and clinical relevance. *Journal of Clinical Endocrinology and Metabolism*,
78:1003–1008, 1994.

Migeon, C.J., and Forest, M.G. 1983. Androgens in biological fluids. In
Nuclear Medicine in Vitro. 2d ed., ed. B. Rothfield. Philadelphia:
Lippincott.

Millet, K. 1969. *Sexual Politics*. New York: Doubleday.

Money, J. 1955. Hermaphroditism, gender and precocity in
hyperadrenocorticism: Psychologic findings. *Bulletin of the Johns
Hopkins Hospital*, 96:253–64.

————. 1967. *Hermaphroditism: An Inquiry into the Nature of a Human Paradox*. Doctoral dissertation, Harvard University Library,
1952. University Microfilms Library Services, Xerox Corporation,
Ann Arbor, Mich.

————. 1980. *Love and Lovesickness: The Science of Sex, Gender Difference, and Pair-Bonding*. Baltimore: The Johns Hopkins University Press.

————. 1983. New phylism theory and autism: Pathognomonic impair-
ment of troopbonding. *Medical Hypotheses*, 11:245–50.

————. 1985a. *The Destroying Angel: Sex, Fitness and Food in the
Legacy of Degeneracy Theory, Graham Crackers, Kellogg's Corn
Flakes and American Health History*. Buffalo: Prometheus Books.

————. 1985b. Sexual reformation and counter-reformation in law and
medicine. *Medicine and Law*, 4:479–88.

————. 1986. *Venuses Penuses: Sexology, Sexosophy and Exigency
Theory*. Buffalo: Prometheus Books.

————. 1988a. *Gay, Straight, and In-Between: The Sexology of Erotic
Orientation*. New York: Oxford University Press.

————. 1988b. *Lovemaps: Clinical Concepts of Sexual/Erotic Health
and Pathology, Paraphilia, and Gender Transposition in Childhood,
Adolescence, and Maturity*. Buffalo: Prometheus Books. Paperback
edition.

————. 1992. *The Kaspar Hauser Syndrome of "Psychosocial Dwarfism": Deficient Statural, Intellectual and Social Growth Induced by
Child Abuse*. Buffalo: Prometheus Books.

————. 1992–1993. Mapas del género y mapas del amor: Nuevos

conceptos en sexologia (Trans.: Gendermaps and lovemaps: New concepts in sexology). *Revista Latinoamericana de Sexologia,* 7:271–77.

———. 1994a. The concept of gender identity disorder in childhood and adolescence after 39 years. *Journal of Sex and Marital Therapy* 20:163–77.

———. 1994b. *Sex Errors of the Body and Related Syndromes: A Guide to Counseling Children, Adolescents, and Their Families.* Baltimore: Paul H. Brookes.

——— and Ehrhardt, A.A. 1972. *Man and Woman, Boy and Girl: The Differentiation and Dimorphism of Gender Identity from Conception to Maturity.* Baltimore: Johns Hopkins University Press.

———; Hampson, J.G.; and Hampson, J.L. 1955. An examination of some basic sexual concepts: The evidence of human hermaphroditism. *Bulletin of the Johns Hopkins Hospital,* 97:301–19.

———; Hampson, J.G.; and Hampson, J.L. 1957. Imprinting and the establishment of gender role. *A.M.A. Archives of Neurology and Psychiatry,* 77:333–36.

——— and Lamacz, M. 1989. *Vandalized Lovemaps: Paraphilic Outcome of Seven Cases in Pediatric Sexology.* Buffalo: Prometheus Books.

———; Wainwright, G.; and Hingsburger, D. 1991. *The Breathless Orgasm: A Lovemap Biography of Asphyxiophilia.* Buffalo: Prometheus Books.

——— and Werlwas, J. 1976. Folie à deux in the parents of psychosocial dwarfs: Two cases. *Bulletin of the American Academy of Psychiatry and the Law,* 4:351–362.

Musaph, H. 1994. Sexual harassment in the workplace and in psychotherapeutic relationships. In *Handbook of Forensic Sexology,* ed. J.J. Krivacska and J. Money. Buffalo: Prometheus Books.

Nardi, P.M.; Sanders, D.; and Marmor, J. 1994. *Growing Up Before Stonewall: Life Stories of Some Gay Men.* New York: Routledge.

National Coalition Against Censorship. 1993. *The Sex Panic: Women, Censorship, and "Pornography."* New York: National Coalition Against Censorship.

Niederland, W. 1974. *The Schreber Case: Psychoanalytic Profile of a Paranoid Personality.* New York: Quadrangle/New York Times Book Co.

Noyes, J.H. 1872/1974. *Male Continence, or Self-Control in Sexual Intercourse.* Oneida, N.Y., Office of Oneida Circular, 1872. [Facsimile reprint edition in *Sexual Indulgence and Denial: Variations on Continence,* ed. C. Rosenberg and C. Smith-Rosenberg. New York: Arno Press, 1974].

Ohno, S. 1978. The role of H-Y antigen in primary sex determination. *Journal of the American Medical Association*, 239:217–20.

Oxford English Dictionary. 1989. 2d ed. Oxford: Oxford University Press.

Page, D.C.; Mosher, R.; Simpson, E.M.; Fisher, E.M.C.; Mardon, G.; Pollack, J.; McGillivray, B.; de la Chapelle, A.; and Brown, L.G. 1987. The sex-determining region of the human Y chromosome encodes a finger protein. *Cell*, 51:1091–104.

Pally, M. 1994. *Sex and Sensibility: Reflections on Forbidden Mirrors and the Will to Censor*. Hopewell, N.J.: Ecco Press.

Perper, T. 1985. *Sex Signals the Biology of Love*. Philadelphia: ISI Press.

Perkins, A., and Fitzgerald, J.A. 1992. Luteinizing hormone, testosterone, and behavioral response of male-oriented rams to estrous ewes and rams. *Journal of Animal Science*, 70:1787-94.

Perkins, A.; Fitzgerald, J.A.; and Moss, G.E. 1995. A comparison of LH secretion and estradiol receptors in heterosexual and homosexual rams and female sheep. *Hormones and Behavior*, 29:31–41.

Pincus, G. 1965. *The Control of Fertility*. New York: Academic Press.

Popper, K. 1959. *The Logic of Scientific Discovery*. New York: Basic Books.

Sartre, J.P. 1943/1953. *Being and Nothingness*, trans. H.E. Barnes [*L'être et le néant*. Paris, Gallimard, 1943]. New York: Philosophical Library.

Sauer, M.V.; Lobo, R.A.; and Paulson, R.J. 1989. A successful twin pregnancy after embryo donation to a patient with XY gonadal dysgenesis. *American Journal of Obstetrics and Gynecology*, 161:380–81.

de Saussure, F. 1916/1966. *Course in General Linguistics*, trans. W. Baskin [*Cours de linguistique générale*. Paris, 1916]. New York: McGraw-Hill.

Schatzmann, M.1973. *Soul Murder: Persecution in the Family*. New York: New American Library, Signet.

Shapiro, D.Y. 1987. Differentiation and evolution of sex change in fishes: A coral reef fish's social environment can control it's sex. *BioScience*, 37:490–97.

Sheehan, J.C. 1982. *The Enchanted Ring: The Untold Story of Penicillin*. Cambridge, Mass.: MIT Press.

Silvers, W.K., and Wachtel, S.S. 1977. H-Y antigen: Behavior and function. *Science*, 195:956–60.

Sinclair, A.H.; Berta, P.; Palmer, M.S.; Hawkins, J.R.; Griffiths, B.L.; Smith, M.J.; Foster, J.W.; Frischauf, A.M.; Lovell-Badge, R.; and Goodfellow, P.N. 1990. A gene from the human sex-determining region encodes a protein with homology to a conserved DNA-binding motif. *Nature*, 346:240–44.

Sitsen, J.M.A., ed. 1988. *Handbook of Sexology, Vol. VI: Pharmacology and Endocrinology of Sexual Function.* Amsterdam/New York: Elsevier.

Slovenko, R. 1980. Homosexuality and the Law: From condemnation to celebration. In *Homosexual Behavior: A Modern Reappraisal*, ed. J. Marmor. New York: Basic Books.

Stein, E., ed. 1992. *Forms of Desire: Sexual Orientation and the Social Constructionist Controversy.* New York: Routledge.

Stockham, A.B. 1896/1974. *Karezza: Ethics of Marriage.* Chicago: Stockham Publishing Co., 1896. [Facsimile reprint edition in *Sexual Indulgence and Denial: Variations on Continence*, ed. C. Rosenberg and C. Smith-Rosenberg. New York: Arno Press, 1974.]

Stoller, R.J. 1968. *Sex and Gender.* New York: Science House.

Swaab, D.F.; Gooren, L.J.G.; and Hofman, M.A. 1992. The human hypothalamus in relation to gender and sexual orientation. *Progress in Brain Research*, 93:205–17.

Szasz, T. 1961. *The Myth of Mental Illness: Foundations of a Theory of Personal Conduct.* New York: Harber-Hoeber.

———. 1963. *Law, Liberty, and Psychiatry: An Inquiry into the Social Uses of Mental Health Practices.* New York: Macmillan.

Tennov, D. 1979. *Love and Limerence: The Experience of Being in Love.* New York: Stein and Day.

Tisdale, S. 1992. Talk dirty to me: A woman's taste for pornography. *Harper's Magazine*, 284(1701):37–46.

Tissot, S.A. 1832/1974. *A Treatise on the Diseases Produced by Onanism.* Translated from a New Edition of the French, with Notes and Appendix by an American Physician. New York, 1832. [Facsimile reprint edition in *The Secret Vice Exposed! Some Arguments Against Masturbation*, ed. C. Rosenberg and C. Smith-Rosenberg. New York: Arno Press, 1974.]

Tobet, S.A., and Fox, T.O. 1992. Differences in neuronal morphology influenced hormonally throughout life. In *Handbook of Behavioral Neurobiology, Volume 11 Sexual Differentiation*, ed. A.A. Gerall, H. Moltz, and I.L. Ward. New York: Plenum Press.

Trall, R.T. 1881/1974. *Sexual Physiology: A Scientific and Popular Exposition of the Fundamental Problems in Sociology*, 28th ed. New York: M.L. Holbrook, 1881. [Facsimile reprint edition, New York: Arno Press, 1974.]

Uncited. 1990. McMartin: Anatomy of a witch-hunt. A forum special report. *Playboy,* 37(6):45–49, June 1990.

Velle, W. 1987. Sex differences in sensory functions. *Perspectives in Biology and Medicine*, 30:490–522.

Ward, O.B. 1992. Fetal drug exposure and sexual differentiation of males. In *Handbook of Behavioral Neurobiology, Vol. 11 Sexual Differentiation*, ed. A.A. Gerall, H. Moltz, and I.L. Ward. New York: Plenum Press.

Ward, I.L. 1992. Sexual behavior: The product of perinatal hormonal and prepubertal social factors. In *Handbook of Behavioral Neurobiology, Vol. 11 Sexual Differentiation*, ed. A.A. Gerall, H. Moltz, and I.L. Ward. New York: Plenum Press.

Webster's New International Dictionary of the English Language. 1930. Springfield, Mass.: G. & C. Merriam.

Webster's 3rd New International Dictionary of the English Language. 1986. Springfield, Mass.: Merriam-Webster.

Williams, G.J. 1980. Cruelty and kindness to children: Documentary of a century, 1874–1974. In *Traumatic Abuse and Neglect of Children at Home*, ed. G.J. Williams and J. Money. Baltimore: Johns Hopkins University Press.

Williams, G.J., and Money, J., eds. 1980. *Traumatic Abuse and Neglect of Children at Home.* Baltimore: Johns Hopkins University Press.

Wilson, C.A.; Gonzalez, I.; and Farabollini, F. 1991. Behavioral effects in adulthood of neonatal manipulation of brain serotonin levels in normal and androgenized females. *Pharmacology Biochemistory and Behavior,* 41:91–98.

Wilson, C.A.; Pearson, J.A.; Hunter, A.J.; Tuohy, P.A.; and Payne, A.P. 1986. The effect of neonatal manipulation of hypothalamic serotonin levels on sexual activity in the adult rat. *Pharmacology Biochemistry and Behavior,* 24:1175–83.

Wittgenstein, L. 1981. *Tractatus Logico-Philosophicus,* trans. D.F. Pears and B.F. McGuinness [*Logisch-philosophische Abhandlung*]. New York: Routledge & Kegan Paul.

Wollstonecraft, M. 1792. *A Vindication of the Rights of Woman: With Strictures on Political and Moral Subjects.* Boston: Thomas and Andrews.

Zaidel, D.W. 1994. Worlds apart: Pictorial semantics in the left and right cerebral hemispheres. *Current Directions in Psychological Science* 3:5–8.

Name Index

Subject Index

Of related interest from Continuum

Rob Baker

The Art of AIDS: From Stigma to Conscience

The first comprehensive exploration of the aesthetic dimensions of the AIDS epidemic. "Rob Baker was one of the first—and one of the very best—to write seriously about pop culture in the sixties. Now he gives us an essential, remarkably concise, analytic yet personal, and constantly readable overview of plague art."—LINDA WINER, *New York Newsday*

252 pages 0-8264-0653-X $12.95

Robert T. Francouer, Editor-in-Chief; Martha Cornog, Timothy Perper, and Norman A. Scherzer, Coeditors

The Complete Dictionary of Sexology

New Expanded Edition

Now in paperback. With detailed definitions of more than six thousand sexually related terms.

"The editors, long recognized as experts in this field, have succeeded in their objective of defining words in the context in which they are used . . . a unique and useful source." —*Choice*

"Well executed . . . a remarkable job."—*Booklist*

800 pages 0-8264-0672-6 $29.95

Sigmund Freud

Psychological Writings and Letters

Edited by Sander L. Gilman

The classic works on sexuality, infant sexuality, dreams, psychological procedure, telepathy, jokes, and the uncanny—also featuring a selection of Freud's correspondence.

324 pages 0-8264-0723-4 $14.95

Donald McCormick

Erotic Literature: A Connoisseur's Guide

"Truly a connoisseur's guide, *Erotic Literature* serves as both a reminder of the centrality of sexuality to human experience and a guide to its artistic celebration in world literature."—*Wilson Library Bulletin*

288 pages 0-8264-0594-0 $14.95

John Money

Reinterpreting the Unspeakable: Human Sexuality 2000

A ground-breaking and essential manual for the complete interviewer in clinical practice. "Dr. John Money was one of my principal influences when I was writing *Sexual Personae*. He is the leading sexologist in the world today."—CAMILLE PAGLIA

252 pages 0-8264-0651-3 $29.95

Dr. Ruth Westheimer

Dr. Ruth's Encyclopedia of Sex

An authoritative work on all facets of sexuality, for home or school library, edited by the internationally famous sex educator.

"Entries address all aspects of sexuality—from mechanics and biology, to cultural, legal, and religious concerns. The range of material covered in this volume is impressive."—*Publishers Weekly*

312 pages 7" x 10" 0-8264-0625-4 $29.50

Available at your bookstore or from the publisher: **The Continuum Publishing Company, 370 Lexington Avenue, New York, NY 10017 1-800-937-5557**